Welcome...

"Digital photography has made it far easier for more people to take better quality pictures. The advent of affordable and highly versatile digital SLRs and Compact System Cameras offers the winning combination of high-resolution sensors and interchangeable lenses, allowing photographers more versatility and quality than ever before. However, while the latest technology helps make the actual capture of images easier than ever, it can't offer you ideas and inspiration on what to photograph. While being technically proficient is important, it's nothing without creativity and the ability to turn your skills and imagination into great images. The easiest way to do this is to try out a variety of techniques, learn from your mistakes and build on your successes. Our *50 Photo Projects* guide has been produced for photographers looking to test their skills shooting a variety of subjects with the aim of producing brilliant images. All 50 of our projects have been designed as step-by-step guides to make them easy to follow and as you'll discover, you don't need expensive equipment to shoot stunning images like those produced in this guide. With themes covering Outdoor, Indoor, Lighting and Creative, you've no shortage of photo techniques to try and we've also a selection of Photoshop tutorials to help you create great images in post-production too. We hope *50 Photo Projects* proves exciting and inspirational and helps improve your photography. All the best!"

DANIEL LEZANO, EDITOR

Meet our team of experts

All our experts are team members or regular contributors to *Digital SLR Photography* magazine. For more expert advice and inspiration, pick up the latest issue available on the second Tuesday of every month. For further information visit the magazine's website at www.digitalslrphoto.com

DANIEL LEZANO
Editor Lezano is passionate about photography and an author of several books. He has been taking pictures for over 25 years and particularly enjoys shooting portraits and still-lifes.

CAROLINE WILKINSON
An avid enthusiast photographer for several years, Caroline uses her in-depth knowledge of Photoshop and creative skills in post-production to add extra impact and polish to pictures.

ROSS HODDINOTT
A regular contributor to *Digital SLR Photography*, Ross is an award-winning nature photographer, specialising in nature and macro photography. *www.rosshoddinott.co.uk*

LEE FROST
A professional photographer and writer for over two decades, with 20 books to his name, Lee is one of the best-known names in the UK photography business. *www.leefrost.co.uk*

50 PHOTO PROJECTS
Produced by *Digital SLR Photography* at:
6 Swan Court, Cygnet Park,
Peterborough, Cambs PE7 8GX
Phone: 01733 567401. Fax 01733 352650
Email: enquiries@digitalslrphoto.com
Online: www.digitalslrphoto.com

50 Photo Projects ISBN 1-78106-013-4

Printed at Benham Goodhead Print (BGP)

Contents

50 PHOTO PROJECTS: SIMPLE STEPS TO BETTER PICTURES!

26 TRAFFIC TRAILS

56 DAYLIGHT PORTRAITS

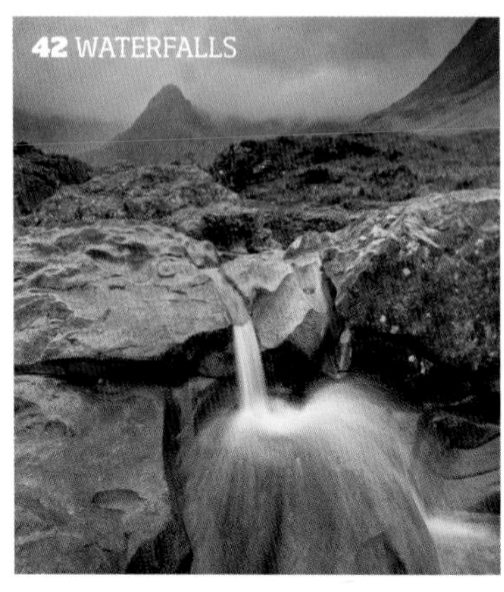
42 WATERFALLS

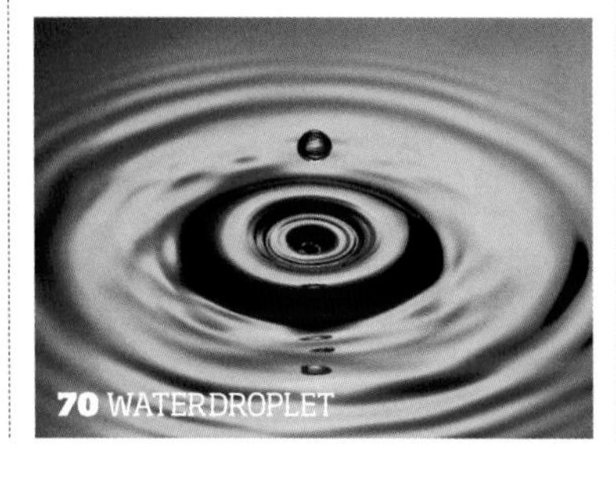
70 WATER DROPLET

12 SILHOUETTES

34 WATER REFRACTION

138 BLENDING MODES

48 GARDEN BIRDS

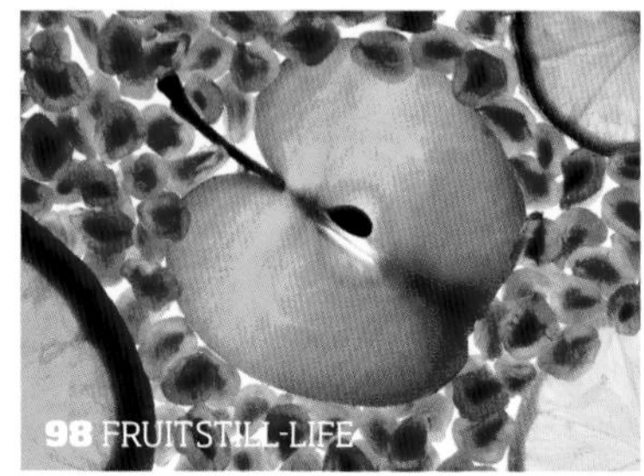
98 FRUIT STILL-LIFE

148 PAGES OF EXPERT PHOTO ADVICE

104 FROZEN STILL-LIFES

Step-by-step tutorials

OUTDOOR PROJECTS

OUR GUIDES HELP YOU TAKE STUNNING IMAGES OF LANDSCAPES, NATURE, CLOSE-UPS AND MORE!

Create 'misty water' seascapes

MARK BAUER: Coastal landscapes are among the most popular subjects for photographers and it's easy to see why. However, translating that atmosphere into a good photograph can be challenging. One way to add mood and create an ethereal look is to use a long exposure to blur water. There's no ideal shutter speed, as it depends on personal taste as well as the size and speed of the waves, but the longer the exposure, the more the water will smooth out, until you reach a point where it appears to be completely still. I like to have some sense of movement in the scene, but how much depends on the conditions and the composition. Keeping things simple often works best, with just a single, strong element in the foreground with plenty of space around it to show the movement of the water. Once you have a composition that works, it's best to stick with it and keep shooting as the light changes so you get a nice variety of shots.

Get ready!

TIME REQUIRED
45 MINUTES

EQUIPMENT NEEDED
CANON EOS 5D MKII
24-105MM F/4 LENS
TRIPOD, LEE 1.2ND (FOUR-STOP) FILTER, LEE 0.9ND (THREE-STOP) GRAD & REMOTE RELEASE

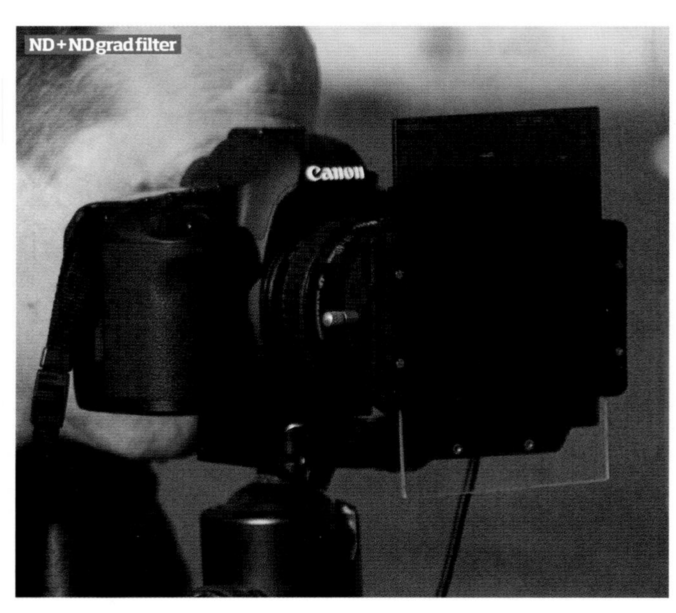

SETTING UP: When shooting near the shoreline, there is always the possibility that a wave may wash around the tripod legs, causing movement and ruining the exposure. Jam the tripod legs as far as you can into the sand or shingle, to keep everything as stable as possible. Once the camera is securely locked onto the tripod, slip the ND and ND grad filters onto the holder.

Essential kit

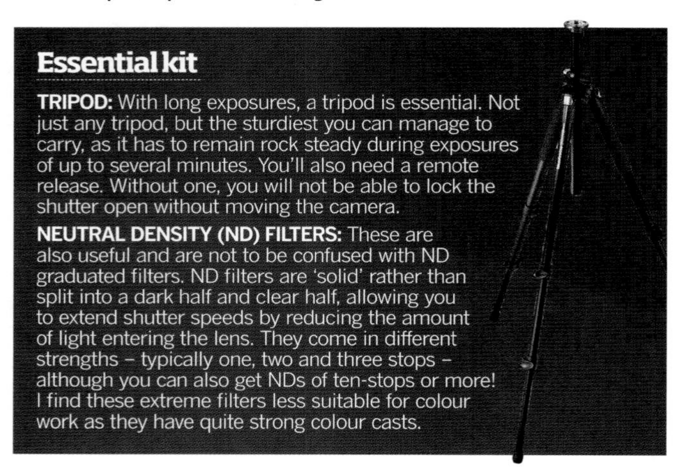

TRIPOD: With long exposures, a tripod is essential. Not just any tripod, but the sturdiest you can manage to carry, as it has to remain rock steady during exposures of up to several minutes. You'll also need a remote release. Without one, you will not be able to lock the shutter open without moving the camera.

NEUTRAL DENSITY (ND) FILTERS: These are also useful and are not to be confused with ND graduated filters. ND filters are 'solid' rather than split into a dark half and clear half, allowing you to extend shutter speeds by reducing the amount of light entering the lens. They come in different strengths – typically one, two and three stops – although you can also get NDs of ten-stops or more! I find these extreme filters less suitable for colour work as they have quite strong colour casts.

Technique watch

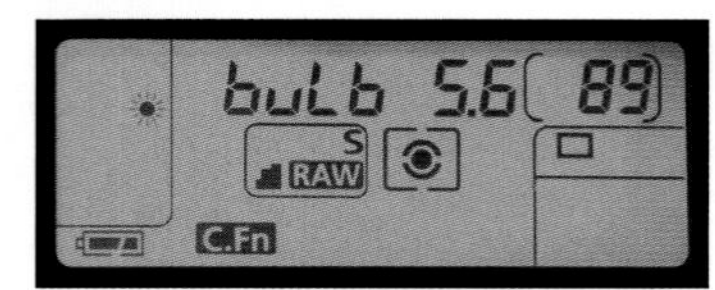

CALCULATING LONG EXPOSURES: When shooting in low light, you'll often find that exposure times go beyond 30 seconds, the longest shutter speed on most digital cameras. It's tempting to raise the ISO and use exposures of 30 seconds or less, but you'll get better results if you stick at the lowest ISO rating and shoot longer exposures. To do this, you need to switch to 'Bulb' mode. You can then lock the shutter open for as long as you need to get the correct exposure. To calculate exposure in aperture-priority mode, increase the ISO until you get a meter reading. Then use this to work out the shutter speed at the lowest ISO rating. For example, if the correct exposure is 30 seconds at f/11 at ISO 800, it will be 60 seconds at f/11 at ISO 400, 120 seconds at ISO 200 and 240 seconds at ISO 100. You also have to take into account the fact that if you are shooting at dusk, light levels will drop during this four-minute exposure, so you will need to add more time. Don't underestimate this – adding just one stop will take your exposure time up to eight minutes in this example! Obviously, the reverse applies if you are shooting at dawn.

1 Conditions were perfect, as low tide coincided with sunset, and had revealed a number of interesting rocks on the foreshore. I decided to include this one in the foreground, as it I liked its textural quality, and the way the waves were washing around it. Unfortunately, a shutter speed of 1/4sec doesn't quite do the trick, as although the breaking wave has created a nice pattern in the foreground, the middle distance looks somewhat static and, if I'm honest, this makes the shot look rather uninteresting.

2 A slight change in composition placed the rock on an intersection of thirds, while the change in angle meant it was pointing into the picture, towards the distant headland. The light had also changed for the better, with the setting sun lighting the clouds from below. I needed to slow the exposure down a little, so I fitted a four-stop ND filter, as well as a two-stop hard grad, to stop the sky from overexposing. A shutter speed of six seconds created a nice swirl around the foreground rock, but the wave is distracting.

Stay close to your kit!
Take care not to leave your tripod unattended. The strong winds and swirling seas can easily knock it over. Digital cameras and salt water do not a happy marriage make!

Final image
The longer exposure has reduced the wave trails in the foreground and smoothed the water in the middle distance and background to reveal the reflections of the sky. There is still some movement in the foreground, and the wave patterns around the rock are still visible.

3 I decided to lengthen the exposure slightly, to further soften the movement of the water, so I waited for the light levels to drop and took a 15 second exposure at f/11 (still using the four-stop ND). I also tweaked the composition again, to leave a little more space to the left of the rock, to include the swirl of the waves in my shot. The longer exposure smooths out the distracting wave in the middle distance, but has caused a confusing pattern of 'wave trails' to appear in the foreground.

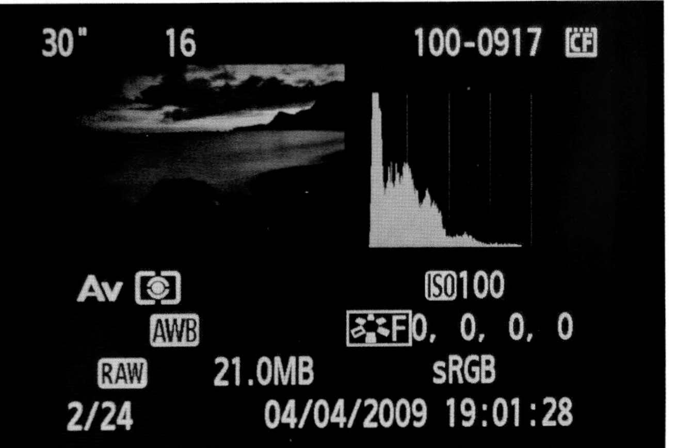

4 A few minutes later, and the light levels had dropped again, so I increased my exposure time to 30 seconds. When shooting in Raw format, I like to expose my shots 'to the right'. This minimises noise and captures more tonal information, and as there's space to the right of the histogram, I knew that there was room to push the exposure further before the light faded completely. For my final shot, I set the exposure for two minutes at f/11 – two stops more than this shot, which would reduce the underexposure seen here.

Outdoor Indoor Lighting Creative Photoshop

Shoot silhouettes

ROSS HODDINOTT: As photographers, we are always striving for the 'correct' exposure, aren't we? However, it could be argued that there is no such thing; as it greatly depends on the subject, the situation, and the effect the photographer wants to achieve. For example, a silhouette can create a truly eye-catching image even though, technically-speaking, it is the result of a poor exposure…

A silhouette is when the subject is recorded as a black outline, without colour or detail, against a lighter background – in other words, the subject is grossly underexposed. It is the most extreme form of backlighting but, when combined with the right scene or subject, the results can be stunning – particularly when the subject is contrasted against an interesting or colourful sky. Despite the lack of detail and colour, silhouettes can convey much about the subject and they prove that there really is no such thing as a 'correct exposure'.

One of the great things about shooting silhouettes is that they are easily achieved and you need very little in terms of kit. I visited Dartmoor's windswept landscape to show you how to shoot perfect silhouettes…

Get ready!

TIME REQUIRED
30 MINUTES

EQUIPMENT USED
NIKON D300, 24-85MM ZOOM LENS & TRIPOD

ALSO USED
SPOT METERING & AE-L

Technique watch

METERING: Your camera's multi-zone meter is designed to render the subject as a mid-tone. Whilst this is perfect for the vast majority of situations, it will rarely produce the results you are looking for when shooting subjects that are considerably lighter or darker in tone. A silhouetted subject can create problems for metering systems. Although highly sophisticated, the camera's exposure system cannot predict the effect you are trying to achieve. Therefore, if the scene is dominated by a black, silhouetted subject, the camera will attempt to render it as a mid-tone by selecting a longer exposure – resulting in overexposure. Alternatively, if the scene is dominated by sky and is very light, the camera is likely to underexpose the frame. Thankfully, avoiding this type of exposure problem is simple by switching your camera's spot metering mode. This metering mode is selected either via a dedicated button, or through the camera's menu system. It calculates the overall exposure from just a small portion of the frame – usually a central circle. Point the spot metering circle at a bright area of the frame and press the shutter release button halfway to take a reading. These are the exposure settings you want to employ to take your silhouette. Pressing the auto-exposure lock (AE-L) button, 'lock' the settings, compose your image and release the shutter. The result should be that your subject is underexposed and appears as a pure black silhouette.

1 When shooting silhouettes, a low viewpoint often works best – helping you to set your subject starkly against a bright sky. Therefore, don't be afraid to get your knees damp and dirty to select a low angle. In this instance, I splayed the legs on my tripod wide-open, enabling me to shoot from a low perspective.

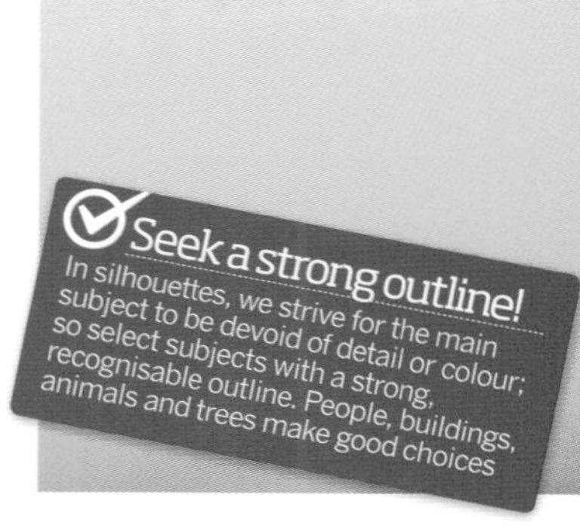

Seek a strong outline!
In silhouettes, we strive for the main subject to be devoid of detail or colour; so select subjects with a strong, recognisable outline. People, buildings, animals and trees make good choices

2 Trees create a graphic, simple outline – perfect for silhouettes. It is easiest to take silhouettes in mornings and evenings, when the sun is lower in the sky, so I arrived at my location early. Two trees together on a hillside caught my eye. Using the long end of a standard zoom, I cropped in tightly to them, but the camera's Matrix multi-zone meter attempted to record them as a mid-tone, resulting in a disappointing, washed-out shot.

3 To ensure that the lovely colours of the sunrise were recorded faithfully, and that the trees were thrown into pure silhouette, I switched the camera's metering mode to 'spot' (this is often illustrated by a dot, as seen in the picture above). On my Nikon D300, I selected this mode by turning a dial, just above the monitor. If you are unsure how to select spot metering, check the instruction manual. If your camera lacks a spot mode, use partial metering instead.

Final image

By zooming in a little from the last frame, I feel that I've struck the right balance in terms of composition. Placing the trees right-of-centre creates a stronger image than it would have if they had been central. Spot metering has enabled me to capture the right exposure in-camera – all I had to do post-capture was intensify the sky's colour very slightly by clicking *Image>Adjustments>Hue/Saturation* and adjusting the saturation slider to +10.

4 I removed the camera from the tripod, via the quick release plate, and then pointed the spot-metering circle at a bright area of the sky. I pressed the shutter release button halfway down, to take my spot meter reading, and then locked these settings by using the auto-exposure lock (AE-L) button. I replaced the camera on the tripod and quickly checked that the composition hadn't changed. Then, using the new, locked settings, I took another picture.

5 Although the exposure was now correct, I was feeling less happy with the composition. It looked a little cramped and I wondered whether I had cropped in too close to trees. The joy of using a zoom lens is being able to quickly change composition without even having to move. I zoomed out to leave more space around the trees, allowing me to capture more of the sunrise. However, had I now gone too far toward the opposite extreme?

Outdoor Indoor Lighting Creative Photoshop

Shooting stars

JOHN PATRICK: Star trails are rewarding subjects that can add an element of magic to a landscape shot, revealing the scene in a way that isn't visible to the eye. They allow you to extend the day's potential shooting time, and to get out with your camera – especially if you work through the week and can't get outdoors during the daylight hours in winter. If there's any 'secret' to the technique, it's getting the exposure right, but that's simple when shooting digitally...

Get ready!

TIME REQUIRED
ONE HOUR

EQUIPMENT USED
CANON EOS 5D
17-40MM F/4 LENS
TRIPOD & REMOTE

ALSO USED
ADOBE PHOTOSHOP

Outdoor Indoor Lighting Creative Photoshop

Get out of the city
The glow from urban areas is known as light pollution and can be seen from miles away on a clear night. This might not be obvious to the naked eye but will show up clearly on a long exposure

1 FIND THE LOCATION If you can, it helps to find your location in advance, in the daylight hours. Midday is a good time to do this for a couple of reasons. One is that it's often dead-time in the landscape photographer's day when the light is too harsh for shooting. The other is that, with the sun to the south, shadows will point north towards where the stars will be circling round Polaris later. Pre-visualising that will help you create a good composition. You'll need to ensure that you're a decent way from major light pollution too.

Essential kit

STURDY TRIPOD AND A REMOTE RELEASE

You'll need to keep the shutter open for the long exposure and the best way to do that is to use a remote release with a lock to hold the shutter open. This helps avoid inadvertently knocking or moving the camera. A sturdy tripod is important too and a wide-angle lens is handy as it helps you get plenty of sky in the shot. Other than that, star trails don't need any particularly specialist kit. Don't forget plenty of warm clothing though. Even if you're used to being out in cold weather, standing around for half an hour or more in the dark in sub-zero temperatures can bring a whole new level of chilliness, so pack a few extra layers to keep you comfortable.

2 SETTING UP Pick your night (a night with a half-moon is a good choice if possible) and set up the camera on the tripod. If it's too dark to see properly through the viewfinder, you can take a few shots with a high ISO and wide aperture, gradually making adjustments to fine-tune the composition. Autofocus is unlikely to work in very low light, so you'll need to focus manually – either by using the distance scale or by placing a torch somewhere in the scene to focus on.

3 USE YOUR CAMERA TO METER THE SCENE You can meter the scene before taking the final shot by taking test shots at a high ISO and wide aperture. I'm using ISO 1600 and f/4 here. Set the camera to manual and start with an exposure time of around 20 seconds. Take a shot and check the histogram, then simply alter the exposure time and re-take test shots until the histogram looks correct. After a bit of experimentation I find that one stop underexposed works best.

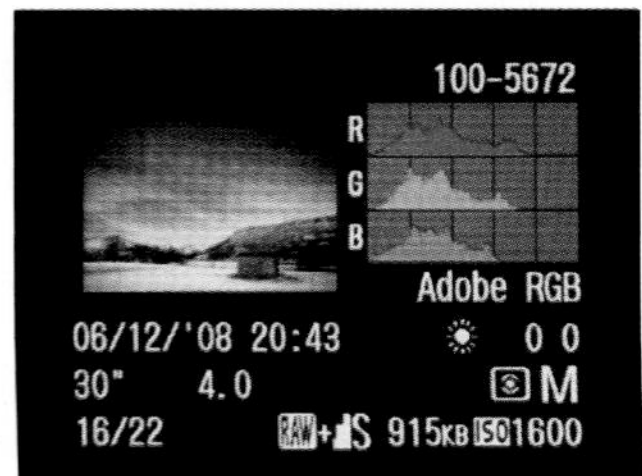

Final image

I've given the final image a little bit of curves adjustment, a colour balance on the cool side of daylight and applied some Unsharp Mask in Photoshop.

4 SETTINGS FOR THE FINAL SHOT When you're happy with the exposure, set the camera to 'Bulb'. Select ISO 100 and set a wide-ish aperture. I tend to use f/5.6. Now you can use the exposure time from step 3 to work out the time needed for the final shot, compensating for the change in ISO and aperture by increasing the time. For instance, if you needed a 30 second exposure in step 3: 30secs x 2 (for a one-stop change from f/4 to f/5.6) x 16 (for the change from ISO 1600 to ISO 100) gives a 16-minute exposure.

5 TAKE THE SHOT Turn all lights out, note the time and lock the shutter open with the remote release. Get out some coffee and chocolate, have a break for a while and enjoy staring at the stars. Just don't do what I did and discover at this point that the coffee's back down the road, still in the car! If you need to put a light on at any point to read the time, be careful not to illuminate the foreground at all, as it will show up in the final shot (unless you're deliberately attempting light painting, but that's another topic).

Outdoor Indoor Lighting Creative Photoshop

Shoot a misty landscape

MARK BAUER: Late winter/early spring is an excellent time for shooting atmospheric landscapes, especially if you're prepared to get up early. As one season slips into another, it often brings interesting weather with it, and at this time of year, misty mornings are common, often combined with a touch of frost. Foggy scenes convey a sense of romance and mystery, and add an element that can lift otherwise bland scenes out of the ordinary. With the right technique and careful planning, it's possible to capture dramatic, atmospheric scenics.

Technique watch

PERFECT METERING: Mist and fog tend to fool the camera into underexposure, so be prepared to add at least a stop over the metered reading using exposure compensation. If shooting Raw, you'll record the maximum amount of tonal information by exposing 'to the right' (pushing the exposure as far into the highlights as you can without actually 'clipping' the highlights.) You'll need to do some work in the Raw converter on exposure, brightness and contrast, but the end result will be a better image.

✗ **Normal exposure:** The meter will assume that whatever it's reading from is a mid-tone, and underexpose the mist so that it records as grey rather than white.

✓ **Expose 'to the right':** Around +1 stop compensation would be enough to keep the mist looking white. I've added a little more, following the 'expose to the right' theory.

Get ready!

TIME REQUIRED
1-2 HOURS

EQUIPMENT USED
CANON EOS-1Ds MKII
70-200MM LENS
MANFROTTO TRIPOD

ALSO USED
REMOTE RELEASE

Essential kit

KIT FOR MIST: Using a tripod is good practice for shooting landscapes, but essential if you're heading out for pre-dawn misty pictures, as exposures can be long. A medium telezoom is probably the most useful lens as its focal length compresses perspective and enhances the misty effect. A set of Neutral Density graduated filters will be necessary in pre-dawn shots, as the sky will be much brighter than the land, which has no direct light falling on it.

1 CHOOSE YOUR DAY: Fog and mist are formed when mild, moist air passes over cold ground – the lower layers of the air get cooled down rapidly to the temperature at which fog or mist forms. Keep an eye on the forecast and look out for cold, clear nights with a light south-westerly wind, as this gives a high chance of mist or fog. Even if the conditions seem right, however, an atmospheric sunrise isn't guaranteed – often, for example, you can get a thick fog rather than mist – so persistence is important. Be prepared to make multiple visits to your favourite locations.

2 BE WELL PREPARED: Mist often forms at the bottom of valleys, where the ground is colder, so the hills above a valley are a good place to be, as this enables you to shoot from above a layer of mist, with hills rising out of it. Being near water also helps, as this helps to cool any air moving over it. Research suitable locations well in advance and arrive a good half an hour before sunrise, as the pre-dawn light can be magical. For this shoot, I set up overlooking the west Wiltshire Downs, with mist lying at the bottom of the hills. Also, be sure to wrap up warm – gloves, a hat and a thick fleece are essential!

Final image

I zoomed in slightly from my initial composition, to remove the slightly distracting band of colour at the top of the frame and keep the shot as monochromatic as possible. I used a daylight White Balance preset to keep the pre-dawn colours cool, and added a touch of vibrance to enhance the blue tones. Keep shooting as the mist swirls around and the light changes.

Mist or fog?

What's the difference between mist and fog? We're happy to provide the clearest of answers – they're basically the same! The only difference is one of density – if visibility is less than 1,000m, it's fog!

3 CHECK YOUR COMPOSITION: You need to look for strong, bold shapes, as mist hides shapes and dilutes colours, making a scene monochrome. I like to look for overlapping and interlocking shapes that help add a sense of depth to the scene. Backlit scenes can also work well, as the shapes of hills are silhouetted in the mist. Flare isn't too much of a problem with backlit shots, as the mist diffuses the sunlight. For this shot, I selected a hill rising out of the mist as the main focal point, and arranged it according to the rule-of-thirds. Behind the foreground hill, the layering effect leads the eye into the backdrop.

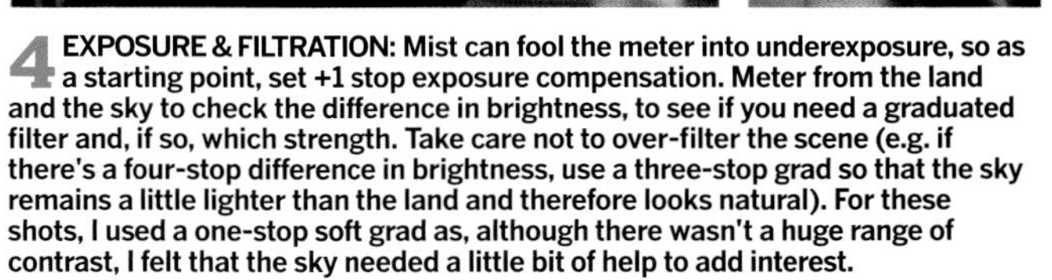

4 EXPOSURE & FILTRATION: Mist can fool the meter into underexposure, so as a starting point, set +1 stop exposure compensation. Meter from the land and the sky to check the difference in brightness, to see if you need a graduated filter and, if so, which strength. Take care not to over-filter the scene (e.g. if there's a four-stop difference in brightness, use a three-stop grad so that the sky remains a little lighter than the land and therefore looks natural). For these shots, I used a one-stop soft grad as, although there wasn't a huge range of contrast, I felt that the sky needed a little bit of help to add interest.

Create poetry in motion

LEE FROST: It's funny how some photographic techniques come about purely by accident. For example, it's said that solarisation was discovered when American photographer Lee Miller (working as Man Ray's assistant at the time), turned the darkroom light on while a print was still in the developer, causing a partial reversal of the image tones. I can't claim that my latest technique will achieve the same level of fame or popularity, but I discovered it under similar circumstances, while taking pictures on the Northumberland coast just before Christmas. I was planning to shoot a sequence of images for a stitched panorama, so I levelled the camera and scanned the scene I wanted to record. Confident that everything was ready, I tripped the shutter to expose the first frame but, without thinking, I swung the camera to the right, ready to shoot the second frame before the exposure for the first had ended. Annoyed by my impatience, I waited for the image to appear on my camera's preview screen so I could erase it. But when the image did appear, far from being a load of old rubbish, as expected, it looked fantastic – an eye-catching abstract of coloured lines and streaks, more like a painting than a photograph. Surprised by my happy accident, I decided to try and repeat the effect, but this time doing it on purpose. Since then, I've produced a whole series of these images. Not only are they easy and fun, but the results look fantastic. Here's a step-by-step guide so you can try it yourself.

Get ready!

TIME REQUIRED
TEN MINUTES

EQUIPMENT USED
CANON EOS-1DS MK III
CANON 24-70MM F/2.8
0.6ND HARD GRAD & FILTER HOLDER
TRIPOD & REMOTE

Essential kit

TRIPOD HEAD:
If you want to produce smooth, consistent results using this technique, you need the right type of tripod head. I've been using a Manfrotto 410 Junior geared head for the past few years. It is great for precise adjustments, but not so great when you want to make bigger, fluid movements of the camera. Fortunately, just before Christmas I replaced the geared head with a Manfrotto ball head, which can be unlocked on the horizontal axis, making it easy to pan the camera evenly. Pan & tilt heads are even better because they have arms to adjust the camera on each axis, so you can lock the forward/backward tilt and the vertical adjustment and simply move the camera on the horizontal.

Steady as you go

Though this technique is all about movement, it's important that your tripod is sturdy and locked off in all directions, other than the pan – otherwise you'll just get a blurry mess

1 First find a suitable location. I live by the sea and favour coastal views because there are defined lines of colour in the scene, created by the beach, then the sea, then the sky. However, any scene containing bands of colour is suitable. In the spring, fields of yellow oilseed rape against blue sky would work brilliantly. The same goes for poppy fields in summer. Urban scenes at night are worth a try too, as the colourful lights will record as streaks. The important thing is that you have clearly defined areas of colour that are wide enough to form strips across your shot. Remember though, that this is an experiment and breaking the rules is allowed!

2 If you want the lines and streaks in the image to be straight (or as straight as possible), you need to make sure the camera is level and that it remains level when you pan across during the exposure. I do this by first using the spirit level on my tripod, and then using a second spirit level, mounted on my hotshoe, which helps me to level the camera itself.

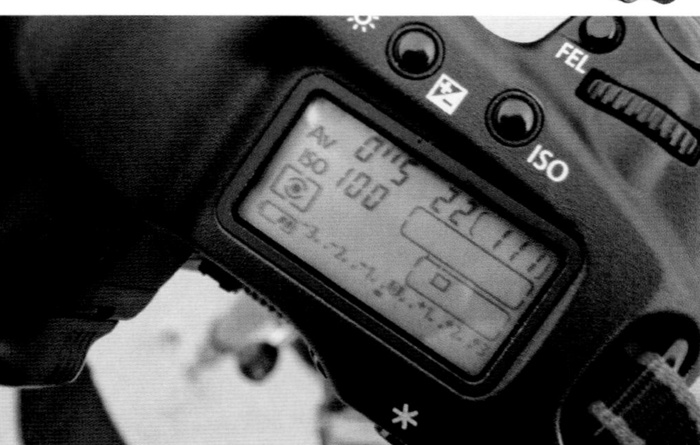

3 The streaking is created by moving the camera during exposure, so the shutter speed you use is important. Anything between 0.5secs to two seconds is ideal. To set this, I set the camera to aperture-priority mode and stop the lens down to f/16 or f/22. In low light, such a small aperture may not be necessary, while in bright conditions I often need a Neutral Density filter.

Final image

The final stage, for me, is to crop the image to a square. I feel that the square format adds to the symmetry and makes the composition more balanced and ordered. By always keeping the horizon central, a consistent theme runs through each image, making them work well together.

4 Once you're set up and ready, do a few practice runs without taking any pictures. Hold the tripod head or adjustment arm, position the camera to the left of the scene you want to shoot, then smoothly pan from left to right. When you're happy you know what you're doing, try it for real. The results may be a little jerky to begin with, but you'll soon get the hang of it.

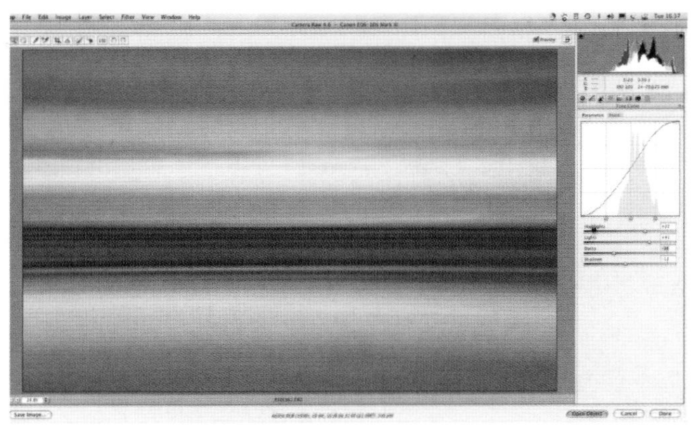

5 Back home, download the images to your computer. I shoot in Raw, so the first step is to process them using Adobe Camera Raw. I usually find that adjustments to Clarity and Vibrance add impact, along with Tone Curve to boost contrast. Once opened in Photoshop, I select the sky, make further adjustments to levels and curves, and then do the same to the foreground.

Wild web wonders

ROSS HODDINOTT: Rather than searching the web for ideas, why not get outside with your digital camera and search for a real web? Spiders spin beautiful cobwebs of sticky silk, and their constructions are intricate, often symmetrical and look stunning close up. Therefore, if you own a close-focusing zoom, close-up filter, extension tube or – better still – a dedicated macro lens, you will be able to capture stunning, frame-filling images.

Spiders live everywhere, so you shouldn't struggle to find a suitable web to photograph. They're easiest to find and look their most photogenic when smothered in tiny water droplets. Therefore, early morning after a clear, still night is the best time to look. Alternatively, you could spray one with water to create a similar effect by using a gardener's spray bottle to create a fine mist that won't damage the web. In autumn and winter, after a cold and frosty night, you might even find a frozen web, which is particularly photogenic and can make very arty, abstract-looking images by using a shallow depth-of-field, together with careful focusing.

Get ready!

TIME REQUIRED
30 MINUTES

EQUIPMENT USED
NIKON D300, SIGMA 150MM, TRIPOD & REMOTE RELEASE

ALSO USED
REFLECTOR

Handle with care!
Be careful not to knock the web, or any grasses it might be joined to (it's easily done with a tripod leg). If you do, you may damage the web and knock the ground photogenic droplets to the ground

1 I didn't have to search long before finding a dew-laden web. I composed the image quickly, including the entire web in the frame. I set an aperture of f/8, hoping that this would create sufficient depth-of-field to keep the web sharp, while not recording too much background detail. However, I didn't pay enough attention to the background and the web doesn't stand out very well against the light backdrop.

Essential kit

REFLECTOR:
A compact, fold-away reflector is an essential close-up accessory. They are designed to bounce natural light onto miniature subjects in order to relieve ugly shadows. A reflector will normally create a more natural-looking form of illumination than flash. However, I have often employed a reflector (or its black cover) as a makeshift background for small subjects to create a simple backdrop. In some situations, you can even use a reflector's silver or white side in order to create high-key results.

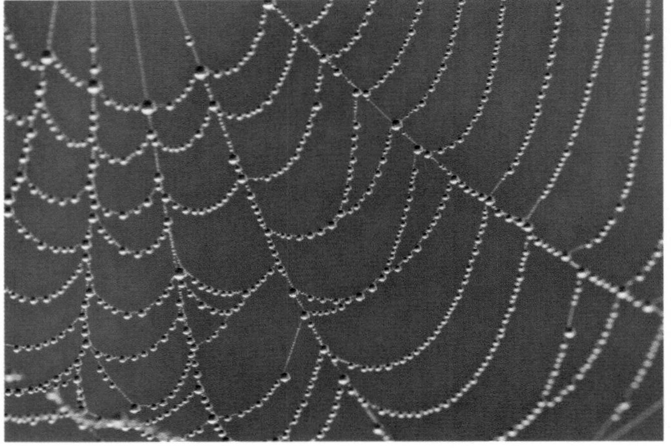

2 The subject's backdrop is often a major contributing factor to a photo's success or failure. By simply changing viewpoint, shooting angle, focal length or aperture, you can alter the background's colour and appearance. To eliminate the white sky from the image-space, I selected a higher angle by extending the legs of my tripod. A grassy bank now created a more attractive, green background. I also opted for a tighter composition.

3 I wanted to create a more arty looking result. So, I selected a larger aperture of f/4, and placed my set-up at an angle to the web. This would allow me to record just part of the web in focus. Focusing needs to be accurate when working with such a shallow depth-of-field. I checked the image on the LCD monitor, zooming in to check the subject's sharpness. Unfortunately, my focusing isn't precise enough and the image is soft.

4 I tried again. Using a shallow depth-of-field at this level of magnification allows the photographer to precisely direct the viewer's eye to a specific point of focus. If your camera has a preview button, use it to review the distribution of depth-of-field. This time I took an extra few moments to ensure my focusing was accurate and released the shutter remotely to prevent any camera movement spoiling the image.

5 Although happy with the previous shot, I felt a black backdrop would suit the subject better – thinking it would contrast starkly with the glistening water droplets. The cover of my foldaway reflector is black, so I held it around 40cm behind the web and used the self-timer to trigger the shutter. Finally, I had the result I wanted. If you'd prefer a more colourful look, you could try using brightly-coloured card to alter the appearance of the background.

Shooting traffic trails

PAUL WARD: One of the most stunning techniques on which to practise your low-light photography skills is the capturing of traffic trails. Not only are there an abundance of vehicles on the road, but on dark evenings from late autumn through to springtime, you can venture out just after *EastEnders* to give this technique a go, rather than waiting until the dead of night.

Images of traffic trails work by combining a long shutter speed with the fast-moving lights caused by cars passing through the frame. Because of the low light and long exposure, the cars are invisible, leaving only the streaks of their headlights in the shot. The technique requires the smallest amount of kit, which makes it even more appealing. All you need is a digital camera and a tripod, although a remote release cable will make the process a lot easier. Ready to give this technique a go, I grabbed my gear and headed out into the dark, taking a position on an overpass of a busy Birmingham road. I recommend always arriving at your location at least ten minutes before the sun goes down so you can take your time and find the best angle to shoot from, and also to take advantage of the sky's blue tint that's visible directly after the sun goes down.

Because you're shooting at night, it's worth remembering a few important safety precautions. Make sure you always have permission to photograph if you are snapping from privately owned land. Remember to be as discreet as possible – you don't want to advertise that expensive camera body to thieves. Finally, because you will be shooting in the vicinity of moving traffic – it may be an obvious one to consider – be aware of the cars around you and always place yourself at a good distance away.

Get ready!

TIME REQUIRED
30 MINUTES

EQUIPMENT USED
CANON EOS-1Ds MkIII WITH CANON 17-40MM F/4L USM ZOOM & TRIPOD

Technique watch

WHITE BALANCE: If you shoot in Raw, you can alter the White Balance in post-production after you have uploaded your images on to your computer. However, if you want to try different White Balances while taking your shot, there are a couple of ways this can be achieved. Either take a test shot, changing the WB in the menu as you go, or switch to LiveView and use the LCD monitor to judge how the White Balance presets affect your image.

1 **I set up my tripod to take a few quick test shots at a high ISO, to see how the angles and lights look, before returning the ISO to 100 and placing the camera on the tripod. I choose to shoot the image in portrait format to emphasise the long winding streaks caused by the headlights, and also to include the tall buildings bordering the road.**

2 **I set the camera mode to manual. You can use aperture-priority mode, but the streetlights can trick the camera's metering system. My exposure of 1/10sec at f/2.8 (ISO 100) isn't long enough to create any traffic trails. Also, the wide aperture makes the streetlights look bland – using a smaller aperture will give the lights a pleasant starburst effect.**

3 **I attempt to take another shot with a longer shutter speed. However, as I trigger the shutter button, my hand causes some vibration to the camera, blurring the image. To get around this problem, I attach my remote release, although if you don't have one, you can simply set your camera's self-timer. Remember not to knock the tripod during the exposure.**

4 **I play around with some different shutter speeds to see how they affect the image. At ten seconds the image is too dark, losing detail in the road. However, at 16 seconds the image is too light, with the light trails burning out. A shutter speed between these two points should give me the correct exposure. You should experiment with your shutter speeds, too.**

Final image
With exposure settings correct, everything falls into place to produce a dynamic image. Why not give this technique a shot?

Close-ups of butterflies

Get ready!

TIME REQUIRED
60 MINUTES

EQUIPMENT USED
NIKON D300 & 105MM MACRO LENS

ROSS HODDINOTT: Summer wouldn't be complete without the graceful flight and vibrant colours of butterflies. They can be found in flower-rich meadowland, along the coastline, in wooded glades and in our gardens. Although wildlife photography can be tricky and frustrating, butterflies are easy to locate and get close to, particularly when feeding. Larger species are often easier to photograph, as you don't need to get so close to them to achieve frame-filling shots. Small Tortoiseshell, Peacock and Red Admiral butterflies are perfect for honing your skills. They're large and common, and will often settle on flowers or bask open-winged on walls long enough for you to shoot them.

Insects are highly sensitive to movement, so move slowly and don't make any sudden or jerky movements. I recommend using manual focus, as it is quieter. You also avoid the risk of 'hunting' as the lens tries to focus, which wastes valuable time. Macro lenses are best for this type of photography, providing excellent image quality and a good working distance. However, cheaper alternatives such as extension tubes or close-up filters will also get the job done.

Most people shoot butterflies from overhead, with their wings open flat; but to create striking, less conventional images, experiment with other angles and depth-of-field. Try shooting them from eye-level or backlit to show the transparency and markings of their wings.

To give you a few ideas, I recently visited some nearby gardens where there were several migrant Painted Lady butterflies. All that's required now is a little patience and luck.

Shooting mode

Aperture-priority mode allows you control over depth-of-field, whilst the camera sets the corresponding shutter speed to ensure you can work quickly and with the minimum of fuss

GETTING PREPARED: When 'stalking' butterflies, you have no option but to keep your set-up simple. A tripod often proves impractical – being too fiddly and time-consuming to position, and greatly increasing the risk of disturbing your subject. However, presuming it's a fine, sunny day, there should be sufficient light to enable you to select a shutter speed upwards of 1/200sec – fast enough to freeze subject and camera movement. When working handheld, keep your elbows pushed in towards your chest to limit camera shake. If you do require the added stability of a support, consider using a monopod, which is easier to position and shouldn't disturb the surrounding plants. Butterflies rarely feed or rest for long, so you will need to focus and compose your image quickly – something that gets easier with practice.

Essential kit

MACRO LENS: It isn't really fair to suggest that a macro lens is an 'essential' piece of kit when photographing butterflies. Budget alternatives, like close-up filters, are capable of very good results. Also, many modern zooms offer a 'macro' facility, which provides a highly useful reproduction ratio of up to 1:2 (half life-size), which is good enough to fill the frame with larger species. However, a dedicated macro is the best choice for wildlife close-ups. For flighty insects, a 'tele-macro', such as a 90mm or 100mm, is a good choice. Not only do they offer superb image quality up to 1:1 (life-size), but this type of focal length creates a more practical camera-to-subject working distance, minimising the risk of disturbance and, therefore, maximising the photographer's chances of success. A macro of this length is also relatively compact and lightweight, making sharp results possible when handheld – even without image-stabilising technology.

1 NOT CLOSE ENOUGH: I began by simply watching the butterflies for a few minutes, observing their habits and which plants they preferred. The Red Valerian was a clear favourite, so I stood nearby, camera at the ready. As the butterfly lands, approach it slowly, gradually moving the camera to your eye. Older insects can look tatty, with faded colours, so only snap butterflies in pristine condition. My first efforts were disappointing, as I shot from too far away, so the butterfly is not large enough in the frame. I needed to get closer.

2 BE AWARE OF YOUR BACKGROUND: Be aware of what is going on behind your subject, as a messy backdrop will ruin your image. With practice, it becomes easier to let your eye wander around the frame while you focus and compose your shot. A small change in shooting position can eliminate distracting foliage from the frame. Alternatively, a wider aperture will throw the background out of focus. However, sometimes, there is nothing you can do other than wait until the butterfly moves to a more photogenic position.

Final image

Photographing butterflies is a challenge, as just as you're about to get the perfect shot, they fly away! After nearly an hour of chasing butterflies around, I only managed a handful of images I was genuinely pleased with. Persevere and your patience should be rewarded too.

3 DEPTH-OF-FIELD: This is crucial in close-up photography. Too much, and background detail will be too defined. Too little and the subject won't be sharp throughout. A good general rule is to set the widest aperture that will still keep your subject acceptably sharp. This also ensures that the shutter speed is fast enough to freeze subject and camera movement. In this instance, after reviewing a handful of test frames, I found that f/7.1 generated sufficient depth-of-field, whilst throwing the vegetation behind pleasantly out of focus.

4 SHOOTING ANGLE: Generally, if a butterfly is resting or feeding with its wings open flat, photograph it from above. If its wings are closed, shoot from one side. Regardless of whether the wings are open or closed, try and keep your camera parallel – if not, its wings will begin drifting out of focus. However, remember that you don't always have to opt for conventional angles. Try shooting straight on at eye-level or from a low viewpoint, for instance. With this shot, I combined the two approaches to create a more original-looking result.

Shoot abstract reflections in water

ROSS HODDINOTT: Reflections can be irresistible to photographers. A still body of water acts as a mirror, perfectly reflecting its surroundings. Landscape photographers often use reflections to create symmetry, but water doesn't need to be still for reflections to be photogenic. A slight breeze will create gentle ripples in smooth water, distorting the colour and appearance of reflected subjects. Mundane subjects can be distorted to the point of abstraction, such as a block of flats, a boat's mast or a brightly coloured buoy. By excluding the subject and isolating the reflections, it's easy to take some unusual, arty images. When photographing water and movement, each shot is unique, with the look of the rippled water constantly changing. In order to isolate the reflections, a telezoom is a good lens choice. A 70-300mm lens is ideal, as its focal length range will allow you to achieve a variety of different results. Shutter speed is a key consideration – too slow and the water will blur. For crisp reflections, a speed upwards of 1/250sec is often required. As a result, you can normally work handheld without any great risk of shake. I'd recommend using a polarising filter. This might surprise you, as this filter is often used to reduce reflections, but it can also enhance their colour and intensity. Now all you need is a suitable body of water and a breezy day – not too windy though, or the water will be choppy.

Get ready!

TIME REQUIRED
30 MINUTES

EQUIPMENT USED
NIKON D300 AND 80-400MM TELEZOOM WITH POLARISING FILTER

Essential kit

POLARISER: A polarising filter is designed to block light polarised in one plane. By doing so, it can reduce or eliminate reflections and enhance contrast. They are constructed from a thin foil of polarising material, mounted between two circular pieces of glass. By rotating the filter in its mount, you can alter the filter's angle of polarisation and the degree of polarised light that can reach the image sensor. Using a polariser is intuitive – simply look through the viewfinder and rotate the filter until you get your desired effect. Polarisers are one of the most useful filter types and their effect can't be replicated on your computer later. Although designed to reduce reflections, applied correctly, they can also enhance them. By removing the reflective film or sheen on the water's surface, the colours of reflections will be intensified. Apply the effect with care though – the filter will diminish the reflections if you're not careful!

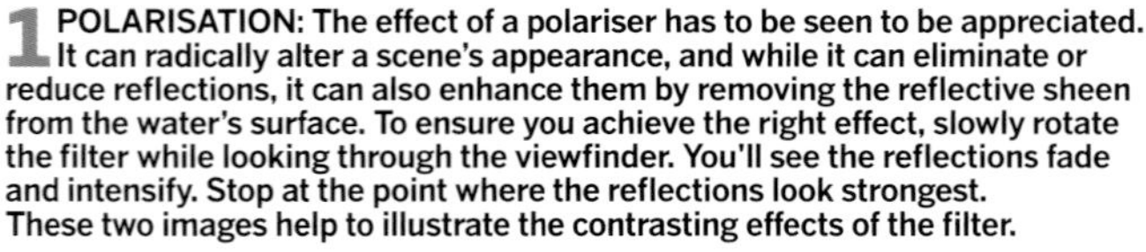

1 POLARISATION: The effect of a polariser has to be seen to be appreciated. It can radically alter a scene's appearance, and while it can eliminate or reduce reflections, it can also enhance them by removing the reflective sheen from the water's surface. To ensure you achieve the right effect, slowly rotate the filter while looking through the viewfinder. You'll see the reflections fade and intensify. Stop at the point where the reflections look strongest. These two images help to illustrate the contrasting effects of the filter.

2 SHUTTER SPEED: Shutter speed is a key consideration when shooting abstract reflections. Too slow and the ripples will blur, which is normally undesirable, as the reflections – and the beautiful, swirly pattern they create – won't be so well defined. A good general rule is to shoot upwards of 1/250sec. Don't worry if you need to select a large aperture to do this – often the narrow depth-of-field this creates will only add to the 'arty' effect. However, this is subjective, so experiment with the shutter speed until you like the effect.

Polariser problems!

A polariser absorbs around two stops of light. Your camera adjusts for this, but you should be aware that the exposure time will be lengthened. If it becomes too slow, raise the ISO to compensate

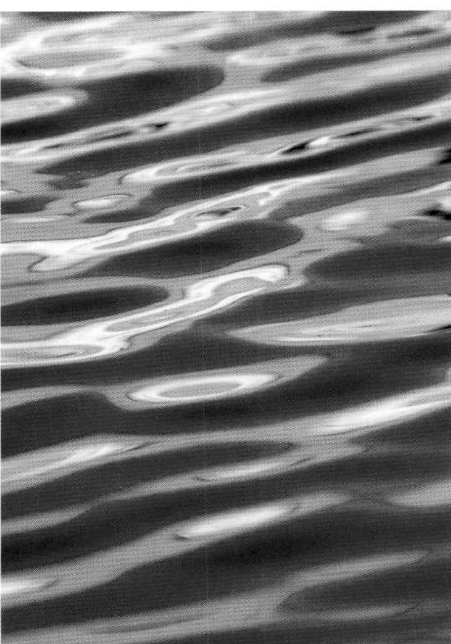

3 COMPOSITION: Don't forget to try both horizontal and vertical format compositions. It is possible to achieve very different-looking results of the same subject by simply turning your camera. If you have a polarising filter attached, remember that switching formats will alter the degree of polarisation, so you will need to adjust the filter accordingly.

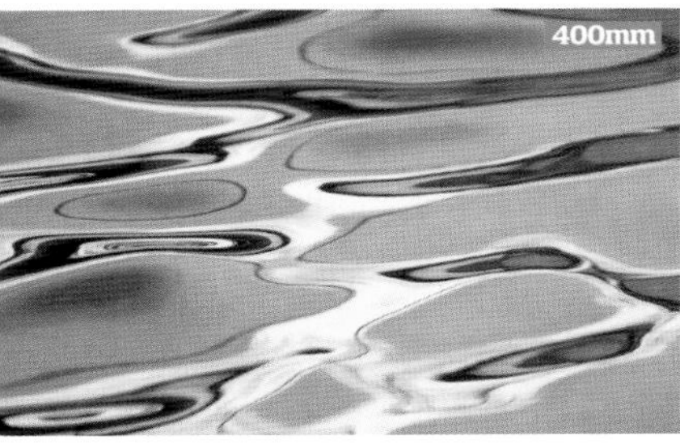

4 FOCAL LENGTH: One of the main advantages of using a telezoom to capture arty reflections is the versatility it offers. You can quickly zoom in or out, altering the composition without the fuss of changing lens. The long end of a zoom allows you to highlight specific details, colours or patterns in the water. These shots show the range of an 80-400mm.

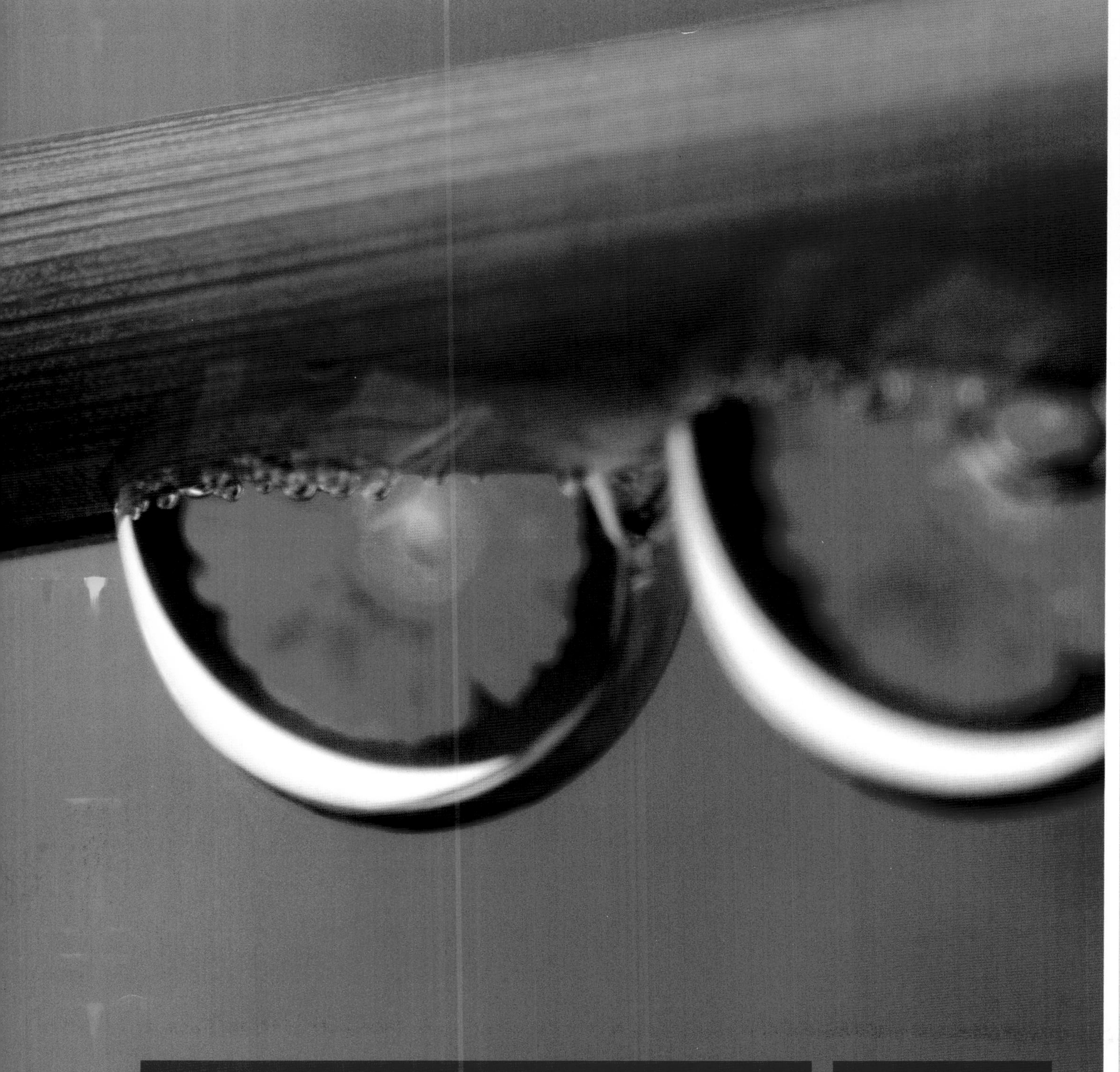

Shoot a colourful flower refracted in water droplets

ROSS HODDINOTT: You could argue that photographing the refracted image of a colourful flower through one or more water droplets hanging on a stem or branch is a bit of a cliché, and with some justification too. However, whilst it may not be the most original idea, there is no denying that the results can look eye-catching. Because it has been done many times before, it is easy to overlook taking this type of shot. This is a mistake, though. There is nothing wrong with replicating an idea… so long as you do it well, and enjoy the challenge of achieving the final result.

Get ready!

TIME REQUIRED
45 MINUTES

EQUIPMENT USED
NIKON D300, 150MM MACRO LENS, REMOTE RELEASE AND TRIPOD

ALSO USED
2x WIMBERLEY PLAMPS, GERBERA FLOWER, ATOMISER SPRAY BOTTLE

SETTING-UP: This type of image is easy to shoot and should take no more than an hour. You can set up in your garden or indoors, using a small table as your base. A macro lens would be the ideal choice, as they typically have a 1:1 reproduction ratio, but a reversing ring, close-up lens or extension tube would also work. A remote release would also be useful (or if you don't have one, your camera's self-timer would help), as would a small reflector. You'll need a nice, colourful flower to photograph, such as a gerbera or sunflower.

The flower and the object your droplets are hanging from need to be clamped into position, and the droplets should be suspended between 10-30cm in front of the flower, from a thin reed, grass or branch. Wimberley Plamps are useful for this, but bulldog clips or tape would also work. Lastly, to create your droplets, use a water sprayer or atomiser. Spray repeatedly until large droplets form and hang from your reed or branch. This can be a rather frustrating process, so it may take a few attempts to get the droplets just right.

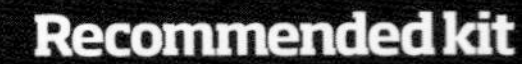

Recommended kit

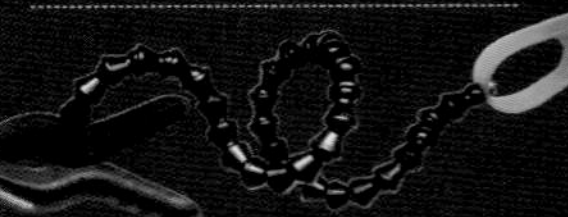

PLAMP FLEXIBLE ARM: I used a basic tabletop set-up and bought a large, red gerbera from the local florist. The bigger the flower, the better, as it will also be the backdrop for the shot. My droplets were suspended from a fresh green reed, from my pond. I attached two Plamps to the table; one to hold the reed in place, and the other to position the flower around 20cm behind. The reed needs to be held horizontally, or the water will run along it, but the advantage of using Plamps is that their flexible arms are easy to adjust and position. I aligned the flower and reed so that the flower head created a frame-filling backdrop. Next, I sprayed the reed with an atomiser until a row of droplets formed. Having done this, I moved my tripod into position – parallel to the droplets and flower behind.

1 Just by looking at the row of droplets, I could see the perfect miniature refracted image of the flower in every drop. I decided to focus on a couple of droplets that were side by side. Next, I prioritised a large aperture of f/4 in order to throw the flower behind completely out of focus. I then focused on the droplets and released the shutter. However, by focusing on the drop itself, rather than the reflection, the refracted flower images were out-of-focus.

2 With close-up photography, depth-of-field is often just a matter of millimetres. Therefore, accurate focusing is critical, which is why if your eyesight allows it, you should always opt for the added precision of manual focus. I carefully altered my point of focus, so that it was on the refracted image of the flower. However, depth-of-field was so narrow at f/4, that nothing other than my point of focus is recorded as acceptably sharp.

Final image

Experiment with vertical and horizontal compositions and alter the shooting angle. Sometimes a shallow depth-of-field works best, and vice versa. I tried several approaches, but opted for a composition at a slight angle to the reed. I then focused on a single droplet, keeping the flower within it sharp, whilst everything else drifted pleasantly out of focus.

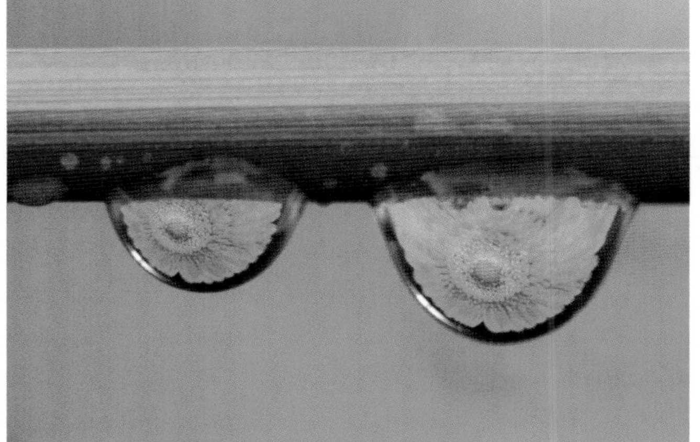

3 In aperture-priority mode, I selected a smaller f/number of f/14. I hoped this would generate enough depth-of-field to keep the droplets, refracted images and reed in acceptable focus. The resulting slower shutter speed enhanced the risk of camera shake, so even the tiniest vibration caused by pressing the shutter release button would soften the image. Therefore, the use of a remote release was essential to ensure a sharp result.

4 The previous image was OK, but the composition wasn't terribly exciting. I decided that isolating just two of the droplets didn't create a strong enough visual impact, so I sprayed the reeds again, to create more drops, and then focused on a larger group. I maintained the settings for the last image, using f/14 with a corresponding shutter speed of 1/4sec. The result was more interesting, but I was certain that I could do better.

Shooting movement in a scene

ROSS HODDINOTT: Using a lengthy exposure to blur subject movement is a popular technique that can create the impression of motion and give images more life and dynamism. It is particularly well-suited to landscapes. This is a very subjective technique, but I think it can transform a good image into an excellent one. However, achieving just the right amount of blur involves experimenting with a range of different exposure times, so it can take a while to get right, and is fairly hit-and-miss. Water movement is the most popular subject for this technique, though it can work well with subjects including clouds, people, flowers and grasses. A golden field of wheat or barley can be highly photogenic as it gently sways in the breeze. On a breezy day, find a viewpoint where you can include a static subject to contrast with the movement, such as a fence, tree or pylon. Now it's time to begin shooting movement in the landscape.

Get ready!

TIME REQUIRED
45 MINUTES

EQUIPMENT USED
NIKON D700, 17-35MM WIDE-ANGLE LENS

ALSO USED
TRIPOD, POLARISER & ND FILTER

Essential kit

To generate the slowest possible shutter speed for the available light, select the lens's smallest aperture and lowest ISO sensitivity. This still may not be slow enough to create the degree of subject movement you require. To lengthen your exposure further, you will need filters.

NEUTRAL DENSITY (ND) filters are designed to absorb light to artificially lengthen exposures. They are available in both screw-in and slot-in varieties and a range of densities. The most common strengths are one, two and three stops – while B+W offer a ten-stop filter for generating exposures of extreme length. A two-stop ND will suffice in most situations. When using ND filters, compose and focus your image before attaching the filter, otherwise the viewfinder image will be too dark. Your TTL metering will automatically adjust for the filter's factor.

POLARISING FILTERS also absorb light – increasing the exposure time by around two stops – and can be utilised as makeshift NDs.

SETTING UP: When using a lengthy shutter speed to blur subject movement, a tripod is essential, or you'll add your own movement to that of the subject. This is a very different type of 'blur', known as camera shake, which is almost always undesirable as it can ruin a shot by blurring elements that ought to be sharply in focus.

1 The Daymark is a navigational aid in South Devon. It is an attractive landmark and I knew that the surrounding farmland was planted with corn. I waited for a fine, breezy evening and visited with the intention of blurring the crop. However, in program mode, the camera selected an exposure of 1/80sec at f/11 – too fast to record any obvious subject motion.

2 Switch to shutter-priority mode, which will allow you to quickly set the slowest shutter speed available for the ambient light. I also selected the camera's lowest ISO sensitivity, to help generate a long exposure. Although longer, the resulting exposure of 1/15sec at f/22 wasn't slow enough to make any discernible difference.

3 To achieve an exposure slow enough to record the wind movement, you'll need to use filtration. Polarising filters have a filter factor of two stops, so I attached one. Not only did it lengthen the exposure to 1/4sec at f/22, but it helped to saturate the colours. I opted for a low viewpoint, to help to emphasise the movement.

4 Although the previous exposure recorded an acceptable degree of motion, I wondered how an even longer exposure would alter the image, so I attached a three-stop ND filter. The resulting exposure was two seconds. However, the movement of the crop was now too great. The corn in the foreground was completely blurred and looked messy.

5 The key is to take an exposure that's long enough to make the effect look intentional; yet without making the subject look unrecognisable. This will depend on the subject and wind speed. For this image, I replaced the three-stop ND with a two-stop ND filter. In this instance, an exposure of one second at f/22 created just the right effect.

Final image

Using the same settings, I took a variety of shots, as no two 'motion' shots are ever the same. I experimented with viewpoints and composition. I was happy with the results, but having experimented recently with black & white photography, I decided the image would work well converted to mono.

Shoot moving water

LEE FROST: Although it has become something of a cliché, using a slow shutter speed to record moving water as a graceful, milky blur is an undeniably effective technique, which is why so many photographers, including myself, like to use it. From tumbling mountain streams to bubbling brooks and thundering waterfalls, wherever you find moving water, the same basic approach can be used to capture it and turn an ordinary scene into a creative image that's full of atmosphere. Even better, moving water is best shot on an overcast day with soft light so there are no blinding highlights to contend with, caused by sunlight reflecting on the water. This makes it a perfect subject for those dull, grey days photographers in the UK know so well!

Get ready!

TIME REQUIRED
30 MINUTES

EQUIPMENT USED
CANON EOS-1Ds MkIII WITH CANON 17-40MM ZOOM

ALSO USED
ND FILTER, ND GRAD, TRIPOD, REMOTE RELEASE, LENS CLOTH

Technique watch

SELECT A SLOW SHUTTER SPEED: The key to success when shooting moving water is to use a shutter speed that's slow enough to blur the water, so it records with a smooth, milky appearance, but not so slow that areas where the water is more concentrated start to overexpose and burn out. This is a matter of trial and error, but an exposure of one second usually makes a good starting point. The great thing about digital capture is that you can check each shot you take to see how it looks, then shorten or lengthen the exposure time until you get the perfect result. If tiny areas of water burn out, don't worry – when you download the images and view them as full-size files, chances are those highlight warnings will have disappeared. If not, it's a simple job to use the Clone Stamp tool in Photoshop to copy and paste water from a different part of the image over the overexposed areas.

1 Because a slow shutter speed will be used to blur the water movement, always mount your camera on a sturdy tripod to keep it nice and steady. It's also a good idea to attach a remote release so you can trip the shutter without touching the camera, which risks vibrations that could lead to your images being ruined by shake.

2 In dull weather, stopping your lens down to f/16 or f/22 and setting a low ISO may give you a shutter speed slow enough to blur the water. If not, use a Neutral Density (ND) filter to increase the exposure. A polarising filter can also be used to increase the exposure by two stops – so 1/4sec becomes one second, for example.

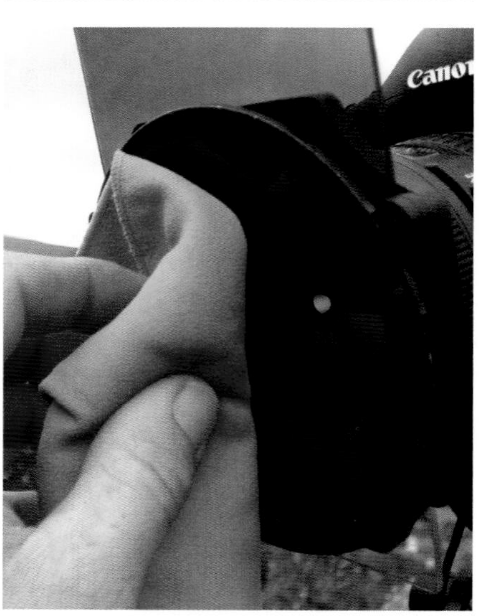

3 Before taking a shot, check the lens or filter for water droplets. If you're shooting close to a waterfall splashes or spray may get on the lens. In this case, drizzle was the culprit. Wipe the water away with a clean microfibre cloth, otherwise image quality will suffer. Holding an umbrella over the camera can help in rainy weather.

4 Take your first shot and review it. I was initially attracted to this spout of water hitting a rock and cascading in all directions. Shooting side-on proved to be a good angle and a shutter speed of one second offered enough blur. The shot worked, but there were many other options to explore.

5 I decided to try a wider view, using the water spout in the previous step as foreground interest, carrying the eye up the ravine towards the distant peaks of the Cuillin Ridge. It took a few attempts to get the shutter speed just right so no areas of the moving water were overexposed.

Final image

Here's the end result, shot with an exposure of 1.3 seconds at f/22 (ISO 50), using a 0.9ND filter to increase the exposure and a 0.6ND hard graduate to hold detail in the sky. The dull weather and soft light worked well, perfectly revealing the subtle colours in the scene, while the blurred water captures the feel of the tumbling mountain stream.

A blast of a shutter that will blow you away!

CAROLINE WILKINSON: David Blaine has shown us he can do it, Derren Brown does it with large tables and, come on, we all believed in the power of Mary Poppins' umbrella. But is it truth or trickery? Quite frankly though, who cares? The levitation effect looks great and, evidently, always leaves people wondering how it was done. Using Photoshop to create the illusion is a skill of its own, usually done through compositing or removing objects that give a person height. However, this time, I'm going to show you how to achieve the effect entirely in-camera, relying on timing, patience, a very fast shutter speed and a subject who is fit enough to jump time and again!

Get ready!
TIME REQUIRED
15 MINUTES
EQUIPMENT USED
NIKON D300 & SIGMA 18-200MM LENS
ALSO USED
MODEL & UMBRELLA

1 I tried this technique in a field and on concrete, but neither worked as well as being on top of a hill with just sky as background. To capture the all-important height, try a contrasting backdrop behind the feet, adding a shadow or standing someone next to the model to benchmark how high they are off the ground.

2 By standing parallel to the model, so her feet weren't at my eye line, it was hard to tell that she had much distance off the ground. Having chosen to move to a hill, it allowed me to position myself below her for an upward viewpoint that really helped me capture the full distance when she jumped.

Things are looking up!
The effect works better if your subject looks up at the umbrella. It avoids any unflattering expressions created while jumping and gives the impression that the umbrella is the cause of the levitation

Technique watch

POSITION & SHUTTER SPEED!
There are two factors that will determine success or failure: the shutter speed and the subject's position. Use as fast a shutter speed as possible to freeze the subject in mid-air, ideally at the top of the jump, when they are furthest from the ground. Watch the model's feet too. If they're pointed down they will mask the distance between foot and floor which makes the shot so effective.

3 I set my camera to shutter-priority and Continuous AF, which continually adjusts the focus on a moving subject to keep the image crisp. I also set the camera to CH (continuous high shooting mode) to increase my shooting rate. You can always try to predict the time to hit the shutter release, but I found it easier to hold it down from the moment she left the ground.

4 The success of the illusion relies on the subject looking like they're levitating. To get this effect requires a fast shutter speed, so I set the ISO to 640 to let me set the shutter to 1/8000sec. This froze my subject but my timing was off so I missed her at the peak of her leap. I tried again, and did better, but her feet pointed down, obscuring how high she had jumped.

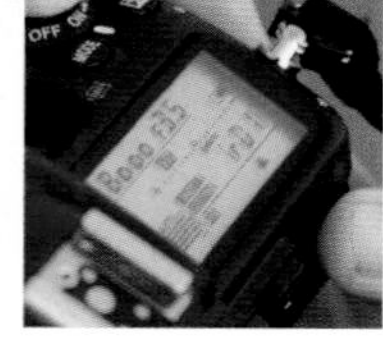

Final image

Timing is everything with this technique. Just keep your subject jumping, don't stop shooting, and you will eventually get the shot you want. I tweaked the Hue and Saturation of this image to pump up the vivid colour.

Photograph our feathered friends

ROSS HODDINOTT: If you have a garden, I expect you also share it with a number of birds. The average UK garden is visited by a wide variety, with blue tits, great tits, chaffinches, robins, sparrows and blackbirds being the most widespread. Wildlife photography is a very popular subject and, at one time or another, most digital photographers will be tempted to try snapping the birds in their backyard. Bird photography isn't easy, though, and can prove challenging and frustrating. However, with a little planning, patience and bribery – in the form of wild bird food – it is possible to capture stunning bird images. You may even be able to do so from the comfort of your very own living room or kitchen.

Get ready!

TIME REQUIRED
THREE DAYS

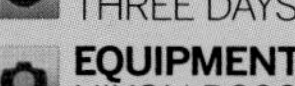

EQUIPMENT USED
NIKON D300, SIGMA 120-400MM & TRIPOD

Essential kit

TELEPHOTO LENS: Garden birds are small and even if you can entice them within three metres of your camera, you'll still need a focal length upwards of 300mm to capture frame-filling shots. Thankfully, telezooms are not as costly these days. The long end of a 70-300mm zoom should prove sufficient, particularly in combination with a DSLR with a cropped type sensor – as its focal length will effectively be increased by a factor of around 1.5x. The only problem to using budget telephotos is that they tend to have a relatively pedestrian maximum aperture, typically f/5.6. Consequently, shutter speeds are slower, making it more difficult to freeze subject movement. In good daylight though, using a lens with a slower maximum aperture shouldn't be a problem.

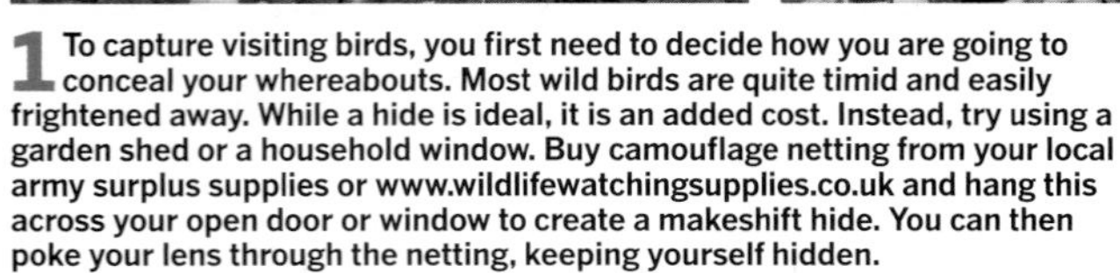

1 To capture visiting birds, you first need to decide how you are going to conceal your whereabouts. Most wild birds are quite timid and easily frightened away. While a hide is ideal, it is an added cost. Instead, try using a garden shed or a household window. Buy camouflage netting from your local army surplus supplies or www.wildlifewatchingsupplies.co.uk and hang this across your open door or window to create a makeshift hide. You can then poke your lens through the netting, keeping yourself hidden.

2 To entice birds within range of your lens, you will need to bribe them. You can do this in the form of food or water. If you already have a bird feeder in your garden, just move it within a few metres of your 'hide'. If not, buy a feeder from a local garden centre and position it close to your set-up. Only buy recommended wild bird seed and peanuts. Within days, hours, or even minutes, birds will be visiting your 'feeding station'. Keep feeders full, so that birds get in the habit of visiting regularly.

3 I wanted to capture some nice, natural-looking bird images. Therefore, I didn't want to photograph the birds on the feeder. Instead, I introduced one or two props nearby that visiting birds would hopefully use to rest on between feeds. You could try anything, for example, position a branch of colourful blossom adjacent to your feeder, or maybe a clothes line with pegs in order to create an urban-looking shot. In this instance, I opted for the handle of an old spade, positioned next to the feeder.

1/250sec

1/500sec

4 Garden birds are flighty – they don't stay still long – so you need to prioritise a fast shutter speed to freeze their movement. Shutter-priority is the mode best suited to this type of photography. Ideally, a speed upwards of 1/400sec is needed, otherwise your shots may suffer from subject blur. Select the maximum aperture of your lens and, if necessary, increase the ISO rating. Despite using a shutter speed of 1/250sec, my first few images suffered from subject blur, so I raised the ISO from 100 to 200.

Plan for the light

Set up your feeding station and 'props' in an area that receives good light for several hours of a day. Avoid placing it somewhere that is shaded by a building, a fence, hedges or trees

Final image

The waiting has paid off! Why not try snapping your garden visitors today?

5 When using a telezoom with a large aperture, depth-of-field will be very shallow. This is useful for throwing background and foreground detail out of focus and helping to isolate your subject. However, such a limited depth-of-field means you need to focus with pinpoint accuracy. Try to focus on the bird's eyes – if these aren't sharp, the image will be ruined. AF is the best and quickest method of focusing when shooting fast-moving small birds, so I set my D300 to its continuous AF tracking mode.

6 One of the key points to taking good wildlife pictures is to be patient and persevere. With my set-up complete, I invested several hours over the course of three days at my studio window shooting the visiting birds. Sometimes I had to wait more than an hour before a bird would use the perch. Be prepared to spend lots of time and take lots of frames before getting the shot you are after. You will have lots of 'near misses', but the good shots more than make up for them.

Capture interesting detail shots of your car

STEWART BYWATER: A fun way to make some striking, colourful images is to shoot car close-ups. Cars make great subjects, as they have so many details and angles, and you can shoot them anywhere, from beautiful landscape locations to just outside your home. Bright sunshine will emphasise the colours of the bodywork, but don't let cloudy conditions put you off. If it's bright, the clouds will be reflected, adding interest to the shots. Either way, it's easy to get great results with minimal effort. Do keep in mind that buildings or objects near your car will also be reflected in the glass or the bodywork though. I chose to shoot a Mini, as they're instantly recognisable, with lots of fantastic details and curves. Many thanks to Alex at Sycamore BMW in Peterborough, who was kind enough to lend me one. To see their excellent range of new and pre-owned cars, please visit: www.sycamorebmw.co.uk

Get ready!

TIME REQUIRED
30 MINUTES

EQUIPMENT USED
CANON EOS 10D & 17-40MM F/4 L LENS, POLARISING FILTER

ALSO USED
MINI COOPER

Essential kit

POLARISER: I used a circular polarising filter on my Canon EF 17-40mm f/4L lens. Rotating the filter meant that not only were the details on the car accentuated, I could also manipulate the reflections on the glass and non-metallic parts of the car, such as the windscreen and bodywork. However, polarising filters do not affect metallic reflections, so be aware of your surroundings, as they will be reflected in any chrome or steel parts. Perhaps the most important benefit of using a polariser for this technique, however, is that they really help to saturate the colours of a car, giving the shots a really vivid look and making them stand out more.

THE SET-UP: Once I arrived at the showroom, I had a lot of cars to choose from. I decided on a red Mini, for its strong colour and distinctive Union Flag roof. I asked Alex to move the car onto a grass verge, so that the showroom and nearby cars would not reflect in the bodywork. I also felt that a clean background consisting simply of the green grass and cloudy blue sky would work better with these shots than the showroom's exterior would. I turned on the lights, as well as the orange warning lights, which I thought would add a little bit of extra interest to some of the less colourful parts of the car.

1 As it was a fairly bright day, but slightly overcast, I set my ISO rating to 200. This would give me a fast enough shutter speed, and keep the noise levels relatively low in the images. I set the White Balance to 'Daylight', although I changed it to 'Cloudy' later on. I used aperture-priority with the lens at its widest aperture, f/4, to limit the depth-of-field for a more arty effect.

2 Once I'd ensured that my camera was correctly set up, and my memory card was in place and formatted, I attached a circular polarising filter to my lens. This is a simple process, as the polariser simply screws into the filter thread at the end of the lens. Polarisers can be really useful for bringing out colours and cloud details. To be honest, this one rarely leaves my lens.

3 One thing that's very difficult when shooting such shiny surfaces as the chrome decals of a car, is to keep your own reflection out of the frame. To start with, I used a tripod on self-timer mode to minimise the reflection, but the camera was still reflected. It also increased the time for each shot and took a lot of the spontaneity out of it, so I decided to shoot handheld instead.

4 In my bid to shoot the car from some unusual angles, I found it necessary to lie on the ground. I find shooting from a lying-down position much easier and more comfortable than crouching and straining my neck. It also allows me to hold the camera more steadily. If you don't want to get dirty, use a DSLR with LiveView or fit a right-angle viewfinder attachment.

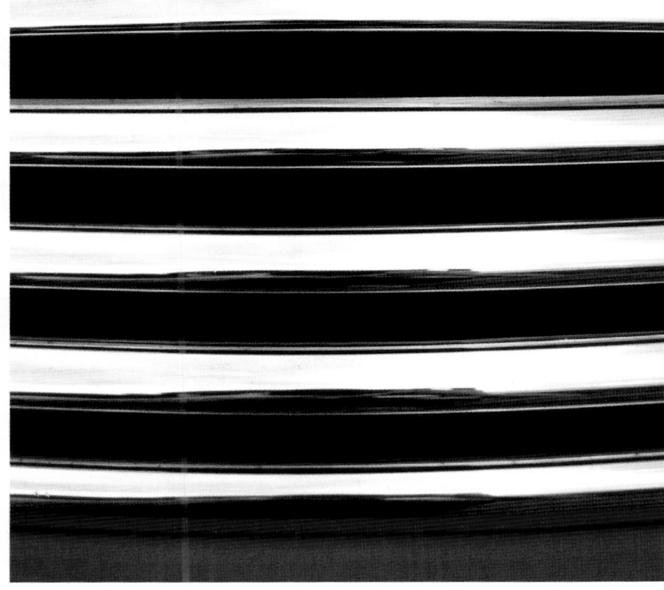

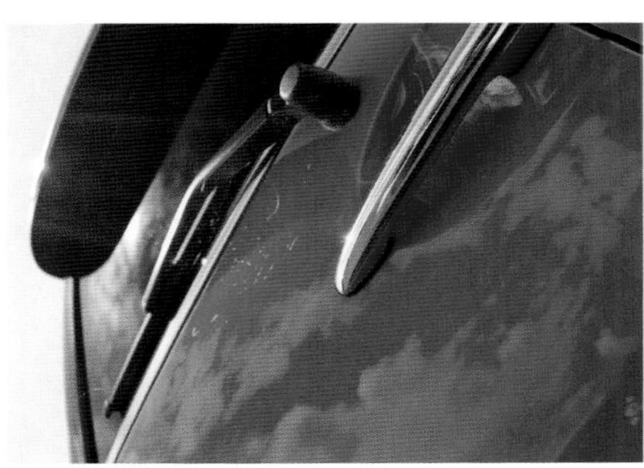

Final images

Because I had used a polarising filter, the colours and saturation were not consistent in all of my shots. However, shooting in Raw format enabled me to adjust this before opening the images in Photoshop. I also added a little contrast and tweaked the saturation where necessary. Finally, I used the Clone Stamp tool to remove the lampposts and any bits of dirt or dust from my shots. I decided to leave the reflections as they were, but these could also be cloned out in Photoshop if desired.

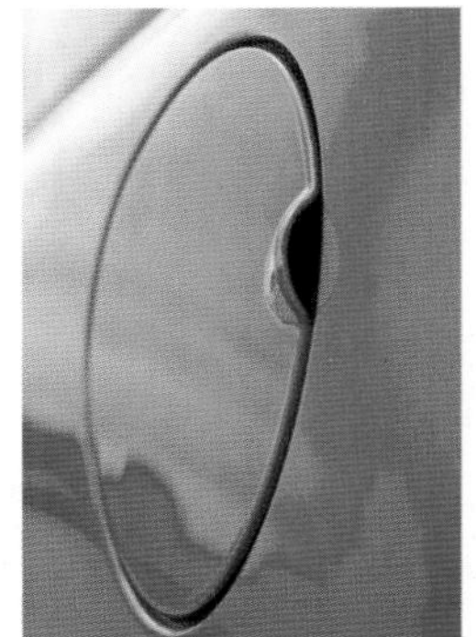

Step-by-step tutorials

INDOOR PROJECTS

SHOOT BEAUTIFUL PORTRAITS, STILL-LIFES AND CLOSE-UPS IN THE COMFORT OF YOUR OWN HOME

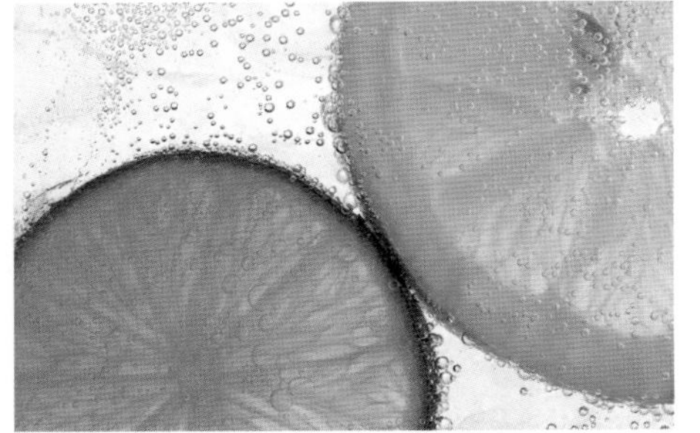

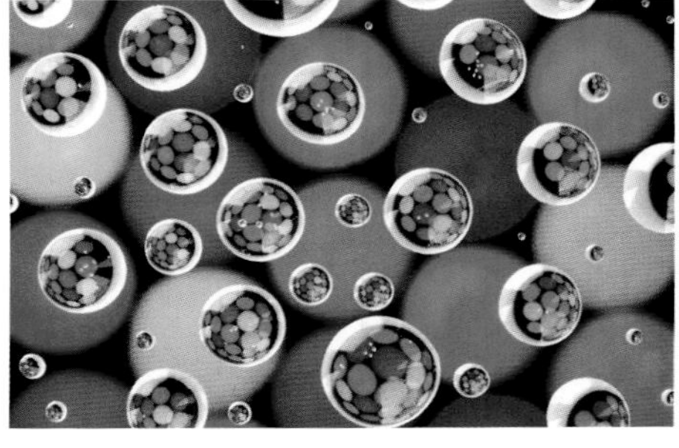

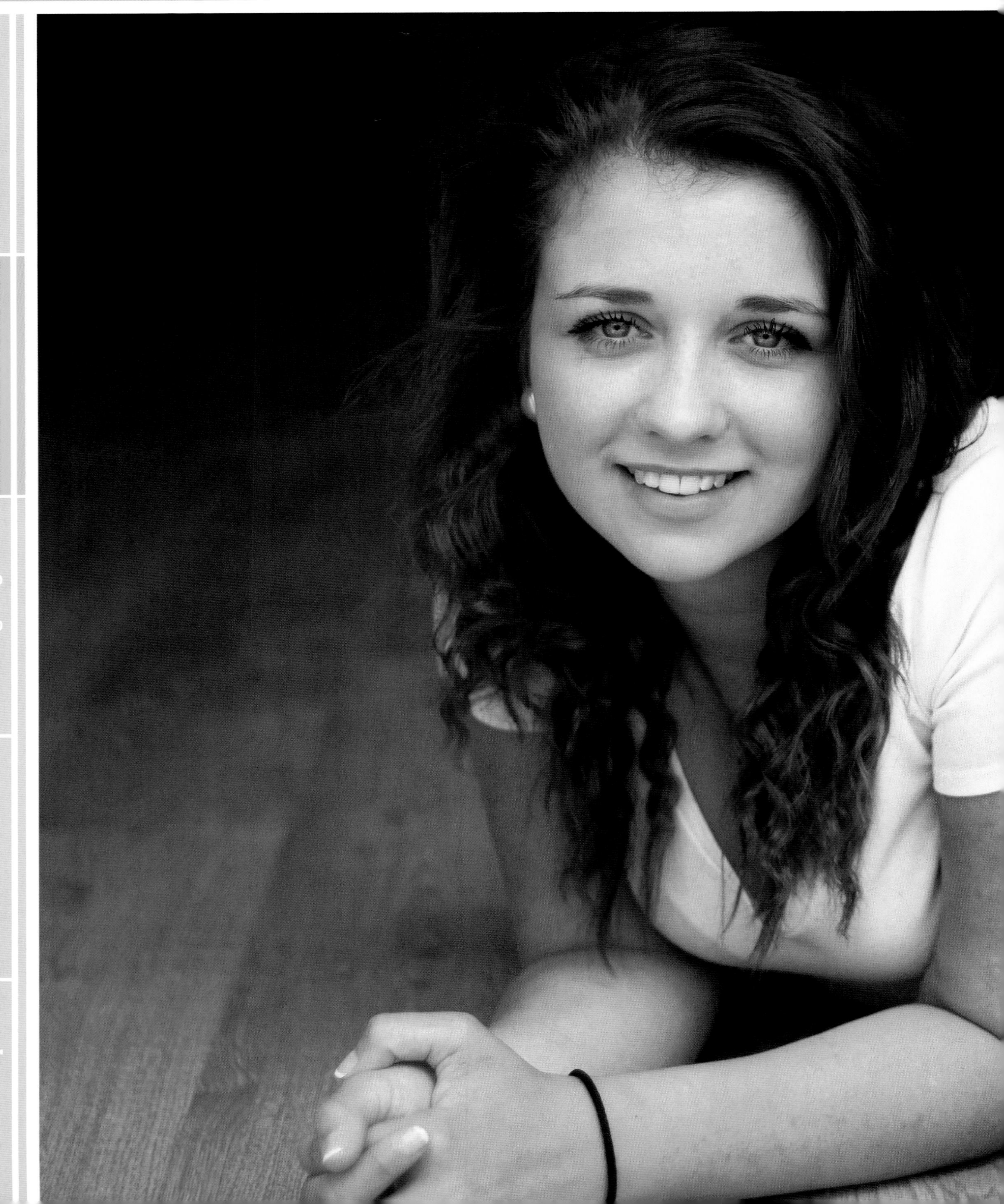

Stay simple with daylight

DANIEL LEZANO: Many leading lifestyle portrait photographers use nothing more than ambient daylight for the vast majority of their portrait shoots. So, while we have the benefits of bright, sunny days at our disposal, we should use it to capture some simple yet effective portraits of family and friends. The best thing about shooting lifestyle portraits is that you can do it with the minimum amount of equipment – your DSLR or CSC with a kit lens is enough – although I'm using my favourite optic, the humble (and cheap!) 50mm lens. Due to the unpredictable nature of daylight, lighting aids such as a reflector and a diffuser can come in handy too, but aren't essential. The key thing to remember is that you want to capture a 'clean' image, in other words try to keep the subject and the setting as simple as possible. I've opted for the classic combination of having my subject, Bethany, wear a white top and jeans, and shot her lying on my dining room's laminate flooring.

Get ready!

TIME REQUIRED
15 MINUTES

EQUIPMENT USED
CANON EOS 5D MKII WITH 50MM F/1.8

ALSO USED
SILVER REFLECTOR & LASTOLITE DIFFUSER

SHOOT AT A SLANT: One compositional trick that most lifestyle photographers apply to their images is to slant the camera so that the images are captured with an uneven horizon. This simple technique adds a little energy into the image and is very effective – just take care not to tilt the camera too far.

Take care with focus!

You need to ensure your focusing is precise as using a wide aperture, which gives limited depth-of-field, leaves little margin for error. Select single-point AF, lock the focus on the eye and recompose

1 My dining room is quite small, so I've had to clear it completely of furniture. As my subject will be lying on the floor, I vacuum it to ensure it's as clean as possible. Due to the cramped space, I open the patio doors in case I need to shoot from the patio. However, I'll start by shooting from within the room and use the white walls as a neutral backdrop. Using a wide aperture to give a shallow depth-of-field is ideal for this type of shot and I'll be trying out my 50mm's maximum aperture of f/1.8, although I'll take most of the images at f/2.5-3.5 as it will improve sharpness.

Technique watch

DIFFUSED DAYLIGHT: For flattering portraits, the light should be as diffused as possible to avoid your model squinting in direct sunlight or having the light on their face too harsh. In this instance, try to reposition them so they're in the shade or use a diffuser to shade the scene (inset right). If neither of these work, you may need to wait until the sun's position changes or shoot when the sky is more overcast. A silver reflector is handy even when shooting in non-directional light to fill in shadows.

2 My first shot is just a tester for composition and exposure. I've a pretty clear idea in my head of the type of shot I'm looking for, with Bethany lying down with her lower legs and feet bent back towards her head. This shot isn't bad, but the side-lighting causes her right side to be too dark.

3 I place a silver reflector to Bethany's right just out of frame and it makes a noticeable difference, bouncing back enough light to even out the lighting on the face. The lighting's better, but the wall behind, while plain, causes the whole scene to appear a little too cramped for my liking.

Final image

My next shot is perfect and all I need to do is apply minimal post-production. I've boosted the contrast in Curves and cropped the image slightly to give me the result I set out to shoot. Give it a try – you'll be surprised just how easy it is to shoot a great lifestyle portrait at home.

4 I shift Bethany and my position so that I'm now shooting into the room from the patio rather than from the side. I close the blinds in the backdrop to darken the background. The empty space created behind her is an improvement over the original set-up but my viewpoint is too high.

5 I crouch down and the lower viewpoint is far better but the multi-zone meter has bleached out Bethany slightly due to the dark background causing it to overexpose the scene. This is easily taken care of by dialling in some negative exposure compensation. I find -2/3EV is ideal.

Fun with refraction

ROSS HODDINOTT: Refraction is the directional shift or 'bending' of light rays as they leave one density and enter another – it is the reason your legs look shorter underwater when viewed from above the surface. The way in which water refracts and reflects its surroundings, and nearby objects, offers endless creative potential for photographers. Water droplets act like tiny 'lenses' reflecting perfect, miniature, reversed images within them. Photographed in close-up, you can capture this striking effect. Colourful flowers look particularly good when photographed through a water droplet – creating an 'image within an image'. You could try taking pictures outside after rainfall or a dewy night when foliage is dripping. However, this gives you little control over the image reflected within your droplet, and you also have to consider wind movement. Instead, why not arrange a simple tabletop set-up indoors and create your own refraction photos? You can have all sorts of fun using different subjects; for example, you could use text, flowers, a flag, a clock or even food. With just the aid of a few household bits and bobs, I decided to create my own water droplet images…

Get ready!

TIME REQUIRED
45 MINUTES

EQUIPMENT USED
NIKON D300 & SIGMA 150MM MACRO LENS

ALSO USED
SWEETS, CD CASE, PAPER & SYRINGE

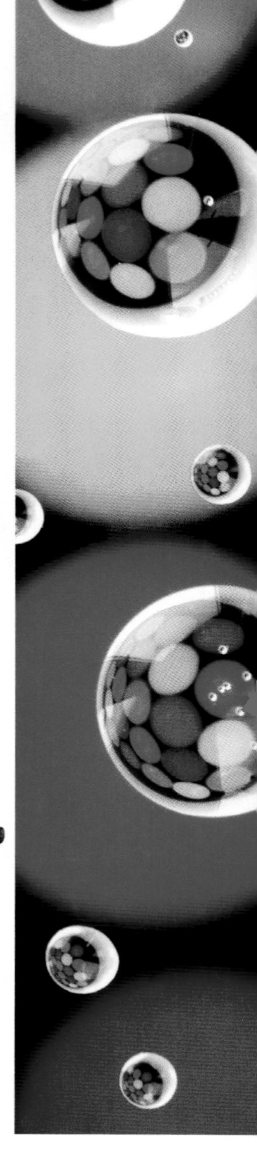

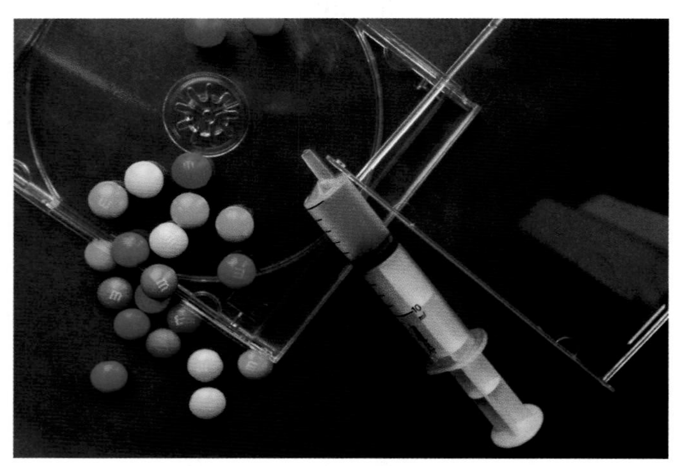

1 I wanted to create a fun, colourful image. So after much deliberating, I decided to photograph the refracted image of some colourful sweets. To do so, I needed some glass or clear plastic to place my droplets on – I opted for the lid of a CD case. To create and position my reflective droplets, I decided to use a syringe, but a dropper or water spray would also work.

Essential kit

TRIPOD & REMOTE RELEASE

To achieve enough depth-of-field to keep both the droplet and refracted image in acceptable focus, you will need to select a small aperture. This will result in a slow shutter speed, making the use of a tripod essential to keep the camera shake-free and to allow you to accurately select your point of focus. Capturing frame-filling images of tiny water droplets requires shooting at a relatively high level of magnification – when even the tiniest movement seems greatly exaggerated. Using a remote release is preferable to physically releasing the shutter with your finger, which can create slight vibrations that can soften the final image. If you don't have a remote release, use your camera's self-timer facility.

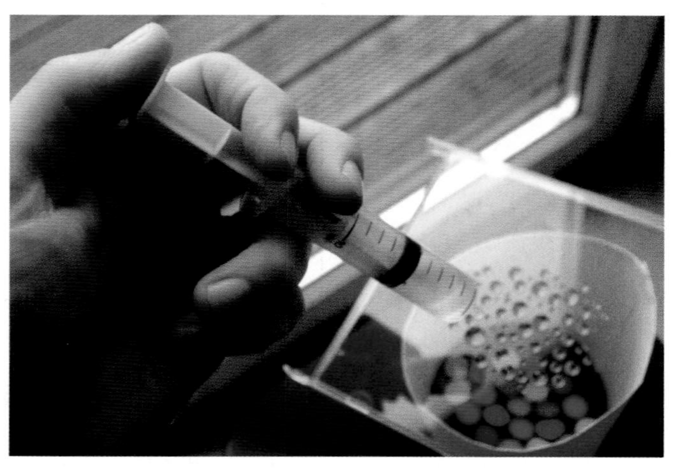

2 I arranged the sweets on a black surface. I then rolled up and taped a sheet of white card into a cylindrical shape, placing it around the sweets, to help reflect light evenly and to create a makeshift 'stand' on which to place the CD lid. Using the syringe, I carefully created a series of tiny droplets on the CD case – each drop creating a refracted image of the sweets below.

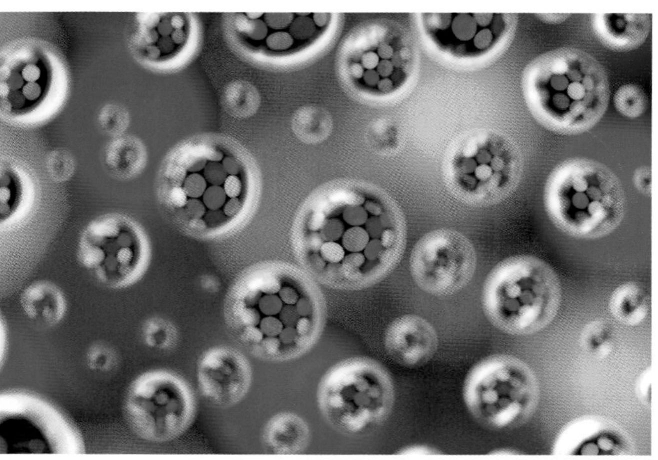

3 Using a tripod, I positioned my camera directly overhead, keeping it parallel to maximise depth-of-field. I composed my shot and carefully focused on the refracted image within the droplets – not the droplets' surfaces. I started with a large aperture of f/4, but the depth-of-field was too narrow and everything other than the reflected images was out of focus.

Focus on the image

With this type of image, it is important to manually focus on the refracted image itself, not on the surface of the water droplet, as the AF system may struggle to predict your desired point of focus

4 I changed the aperture to f/22 to increase depth-of-field. The resulting shutter speed was two seconds, so a tripod and remote release proved essential. The result had far more impact – the droplets were in focus, and the sweets behind made a colourful background. However, dust and scratches on the plastic were also now visible because of the smaller aperture.

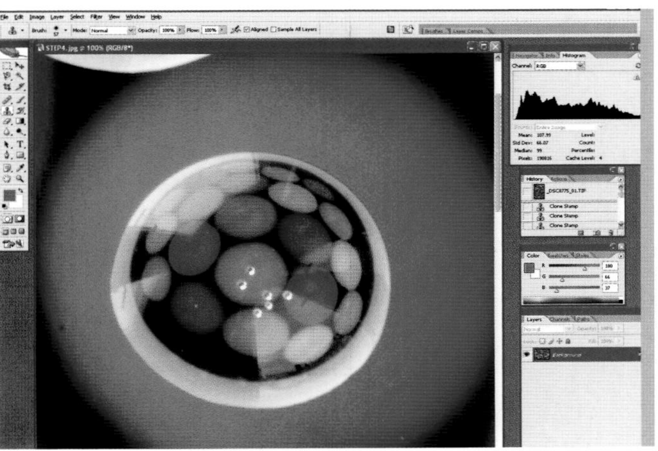

5 The next step was to tidy up my image. Even though I had wiped over the plastic case before I began shooting, tiny marks were obvious across the image. Using a combination of Photoshop's Clone tool and Healing Brush, I carefully cleaned the image. I then adjusted the Levels to increase contrast, upping the saturation slightly too, in Hue/Saturation, to add impact.

Outdoor Indoor Lighting Creative Photoshop

Capture a rose's beauty

DANIEL LEZANO: If you've never tried photographing a flower, I'd suggest you give it a go. As a photographer who has concentrated mainly on portraiture, the enjoyment I found from composing my first ever flower still-life came as nothing short of a revelation. It's an incredibly rewarding form of photography, which allows you to practise your skills with composition and lighting, as well as testing your creativity by trying to find different angles and viewpoints to shoot from. The sheer variety of beautiful flowers available will give you endless options for your still-life. My personal favourite is the gerbera, but it is run a close second by the elegant beauty of the rose. However, I find the gerbera to be a far easier flower to photograph, as its shape allows you to capture it from all sorts of angles and crops. In my view, the rose is a much harder proposition; it is more fragile and the folds of its petals can mean that not every one you find is a suitable subject for photography. In the past, when I've bought roses, I've specifically headed to a good florist and delved through their selection for the perfect subject. For this step-by-step, however, I snipped roses from a neighbour's garden (with permission of course!) to show that it is possible to find a suitable subject even among ordinary flowers from the garden.

THE SET-UP: The great thing about close-up flower photography is you don't need an elaborate set-up. The area close to the French doors in my dining room provided all the light I needed for the shoot. The rose was balanced in a half-filled plastic water bottle to hold it in position, while my camera with macro lens is set up on a tripod. I find that shooting a flower indoors offers two key advantages: wind blowing the flower isn't an issue and shooting in the shade provides a far gentler light. Finally, it's worth keeping a silver reflector on hand should you need to bounce some light back into the scene.

Get ready!

TIME REQUIRED
30 MINUTES

EQUIPMENT USED
CANON EOS 500D & 100MM MACRO LENS MANFROTTO 055MF4 TRIPOD WITH RC322 HEAD & REFLECTOR

ALSO USED
PINK GARDEN ROSE

Essential kit

MACRO LENS & TRIPOD: Because we're trying to fill the frame with a very small subject, a macro lens is pretty much an essential bit of kit. It will allow you to focus within a few centimetres from your subject and exclude the background from the frame, so that the entire image is filled with your flower. Now it's fair to say that you can get away with shooting handheld here, especially if your camera or lens has an image stabilisation facility, but I'd highly recommend that you do use a tripod. Using one will allow you to fine-tune your compositions, ensure your focusing is absolutely precise (this is absolutely critical with macro photography) and also let you shoot a series of identical shots at different aperture settings so that you can later choose the one that you prefer.

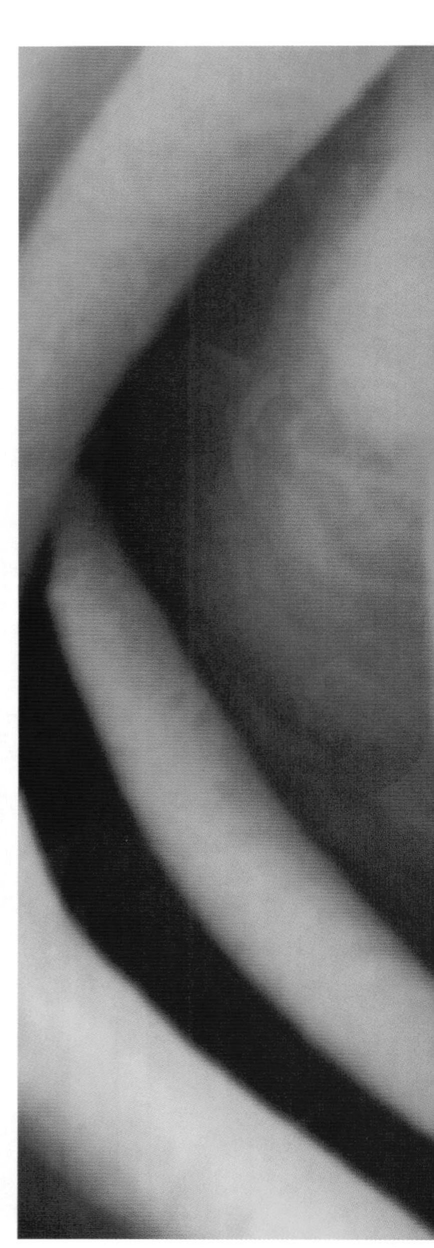

1 FOCUS PROBLEMS I set aperture-priority mode and, for optimum quality, a low ISO of 100. One thing I haven't set yet is the autofocus. I leave it at multi-point, just to demonstrate what happens. With all AF points active, the camera focuses on the closest part of the subject, which is on the far left of the frame. Switching to single-point AF and setting the AF point over the area I want to focus sorts this out. Another option is to use manual focus.

2 FINE-TUNE THE COMPOSITION With focusing solved, take a shot and check the histogram. You should find that unless the flower is very light or dark, your exposures are correct. Now concentrate on the composition. Make small adjustments to the tripod head, raise or lower the legs and move the flower until you're happy with how it's framed. LiveView proves very useful, as you can monitor changes more easily than if using the viewfinder.

Final image

The advantage of buying from a florist is that your subject will have fewer imperfections. This garden rose had a few discoloured areas, but they were easily cleaned up with the Healing Brush Tool in Photoshop. After 15 minutes of photography and five minutes of Photoshop, I've a beautiful still-life of a flower to add to my colourful collection!

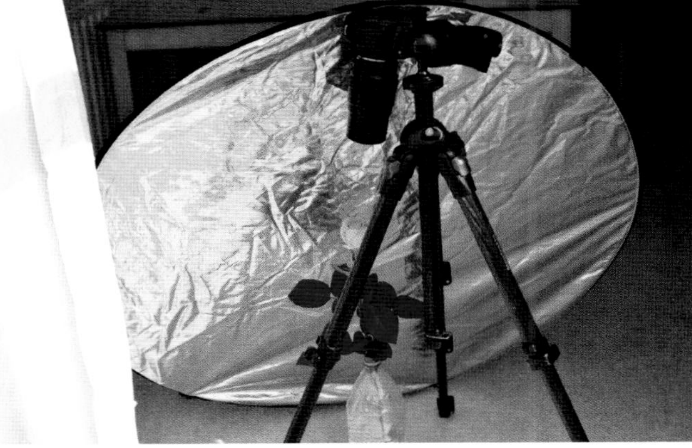

3 **USE A REFLECTOR IF REQUIRED** I was pleased with the composition of the image, but not so happy that the side of the flower closest to the window was much brighter than the right side. I balanced this out by resting my reflector on the tripod leg closest to the flower. The light it bounces back is subtle, but I'm happy with the difference it makes to the image.

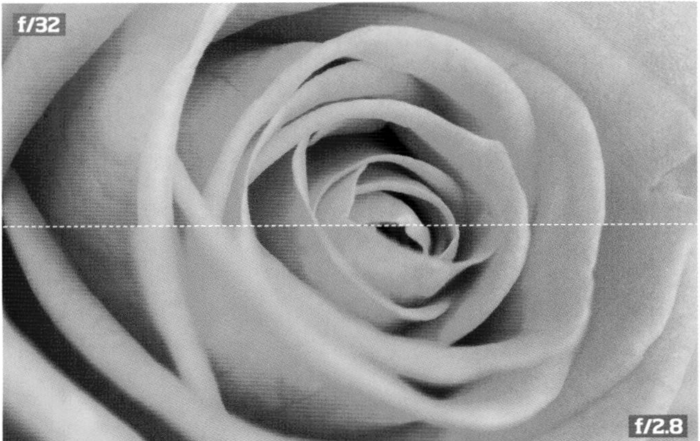

4 **APERTURE SETTINGS** Once you're happy with the composition and lighting, take a series of exposures at one-stop intervals from maximum to minimum aperture to give you a complete set, from minimal depth-of-field to as much as possible in focus. To minimise shake in the longer exposures, use the self-timer or a remote release to fire the shutter.

How to take a perfect bath-time portrait

ROSS HODDINOTT: Whilst some photographers might have access to a studio, or own a home studio set-up and lights, the majority of us don't. So what can we do when we're stuck at home on a cold, wet winter day, to create studio-like results? Well, have you ever considered using your bath? No, not for a relaxing soak, but to reflect light. A white tub will act like a large reflector – reflecting light entering through an adjacent window (or a burst of flash), evenly around a subject placed in the bath. It will also form a clean, white backdrop – helping create attractive, high-key results. To put this theory to the test, I decided to take some fresh portraits of my two-year-old daughter; but would she stay still long enough for me to take a good picture?

Get ready!

TIME REQUIRED
30 MINUTES

EQUIPMENT USED
NIKON D300 & 105MM MACRO LENS

ALSO USED
WHITE BATH

Window light

Window light can often prove to be the perfect way of lighting your portraits. In fact, there are a great many professional portrait photographers who swear by it, only introducing flash as a last resort

Essential kit

MACRO LENS: The only limitation of using a bath as a makeshift 'reflector' is the size of the subjects that you can shoot. They mustn't exceed the height of the tub, so select an object which isn't too big. Due to the type or size of the subjects you will be shooting, a focal length in the region of 100-150mm is ideally suited. A macro lens is ideal, due to its close focusing ability. To photograph my daughter, I used a Sigma 105mm macro. This is a popular lens with portrait photographers, as it allows you to take pictures from a comfortable distance away from your sitter, while its f/2.8 maximum aperture creates a bright viewfinder image.

Technique watch

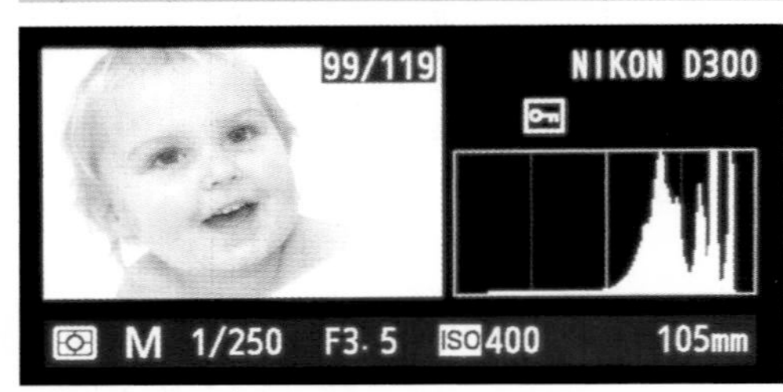

HISTOGRAMS: Regularly check your image's histogram to ensure exposure is accurate. Whilst photographing my daughter in the bath, I relied on the histogram to ensure that the bright, white bath tub wasn't fooling my metering into underexposure – something which would have been indicated by peaks to the left of the graph.

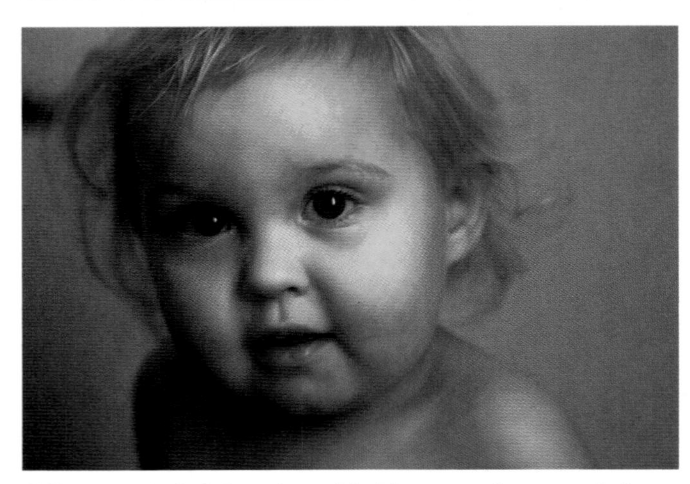

1 I'm not a portrait photographer and don't have access to a proper studio, so when I take pictures indoors, I have to improvise. I wanted to take some fresh shots of my daughter but the initial results were disappointing. When simply taking shots of her in our lounge at home, dark, unflattering shadows formed underneath her eyes, mouth and chin.

2 With the help of a few chocolate buttons, my daughter sat in the bath. Although confused by the lack of water, she happily smiled while I began taking pictures. The light entering through the window bounced around the bath, creating a more flattering light source. The tub formed a clean, simple backdrop, but her eyes lacked a catchlight – vital for creating depth and life.

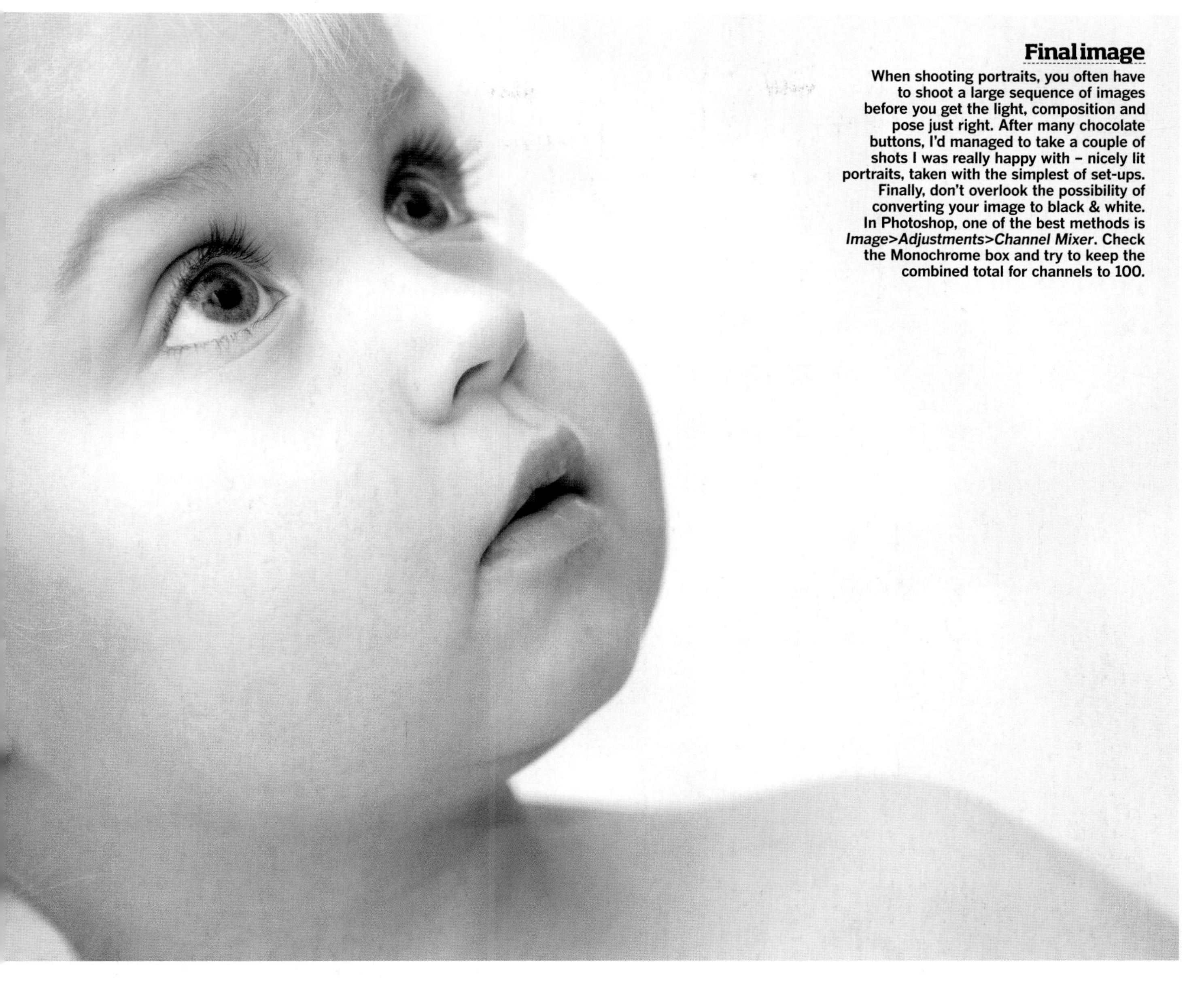

Final image

When shooting portraits, you often have to shoot a large sequence of images before you get the light, composition and pose just right. After many chocolate buttons, I'd managed to take a couple of shots I was really happy with – nicely lit portraits, taken with the simplest of set-ups. Finally, don't overlook the possibility of converting your image to black & white. In Photoshop, one of the best methods is *Image>Adjustments>Channel Mixer*. Check the Monochrome box and try to keep the combined total for channels to 100.

3 To create a catchlight, I employed a small burst of fill-flash. I used my Nikon D300's built-in unit, with a flash exposure compensation of -2 stops, to ensure the burst didn't overwhelm the ambient light. Not only did the burst create a catchlight, but it bounced more light around the bathtub. However, this time my focusing let me down – the eyes are not critically sharp.

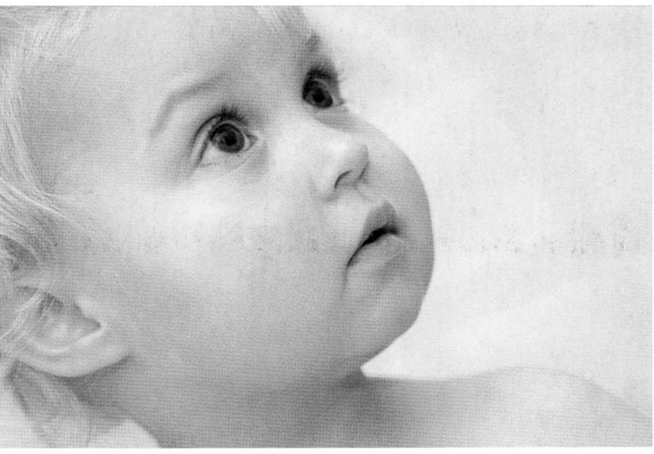

4 I selected the lens's largest aperture of f2/8 to throw the tub out of focus, so it was unrecognisable, and to give a fast enough shutter speed to allow me to work handheld. However, the resulting depth-of-field was narrow, making accurate focusing critical. It is essential that eyes are sharp, so I tried again, taking extra care to ensure the eye closest to me was sharply focused.

Alphabet soup

ROSS HODDINOTT: I possess a complete lack of culinary skills… just ask my poor wife! I'm hopeless in the kitchen, which is why it is safer for everyone concerned if I photograph food rather than prepare it for eating! Opening a tin of beans or soup is just about my limit. My little girls love alphabet spaghetti and it was watching my older daughter making words with the letters that got me thinking about the picture potential. I decided to raid the cupboard and have fun spelling out specific words using the alphabet soup. This is a fun shot to try and it couldn't be easier or cheaper to do. You can buy a couple of small tins for under a pound at your local supermarket, and then all that is required are a few everyday household bits and pieces. I used a small still-life table to arrange my set-up, although a simple tabletop set-up in your kitchen or living room would do the job equally well. Rather than using flash, the soft natural light from an adjacent window is ideally suited to this type of still-life image. Time to start spelling…

Get ready!

TIME REQUIRED
45 MINUTES

EQUIPMENT USED
NIKON D300, SIGMA 105MM, TRIPOD

ALSO USED
SPOON, DISH, TWEEZERS AND TIN OF ALPHABET SOUP

GETTING STARTED: I used a white products table as my base, but any table or kitchen surface will work well. Keep some kitchen towel nearby too: alphabet soup is messy stuff and easy to get on your hands when you are picking out and arranging your letters with tweezers. You don't want to transfer tomato sauce from your hand to your valuable camera gear!

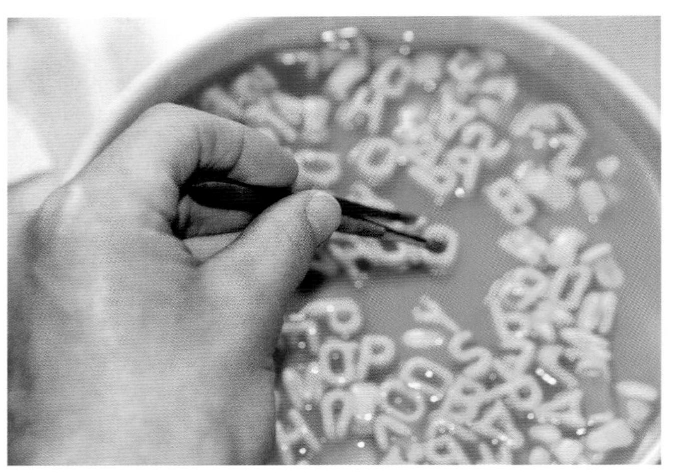

1 Firstly, I opened the tin of soup and poured the contents into a flat, white dish. Using tweezers, I began picking out the letters I required. In this instance, I thought it apt to spell out PHOTO DIY. However, even with tweezers, you have to be gentle not to damage or break the letters, but after a few minutes, I soon found the letters I needed for my chosen phrase.

2 I thought it would be fun to have my words on a spoon as it would help the letters stand out and the spoon would add visual interest. Again using tweezers, I arranged the letters. However, while the idea was good, in practice the letters all slid together as the metal is scooped, distorting their shape and making the words tricky to read.

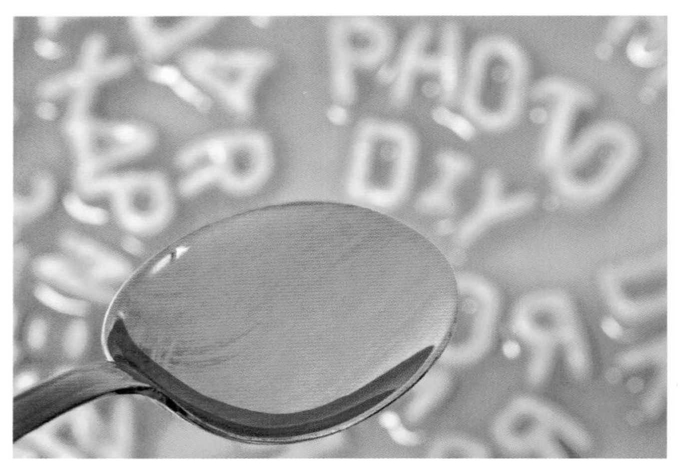

3 Carefully, I moved the letters back onto the dish. To ensure PHOTO DIY stood out I left a small gap around the words. I then held the spoon in position, just above the dish, using a clamp. I focused on the spoon, but to ensure the words in the background were still distinguishable, I selected an aperture of f/11 to provide sufficient depth-of-field.

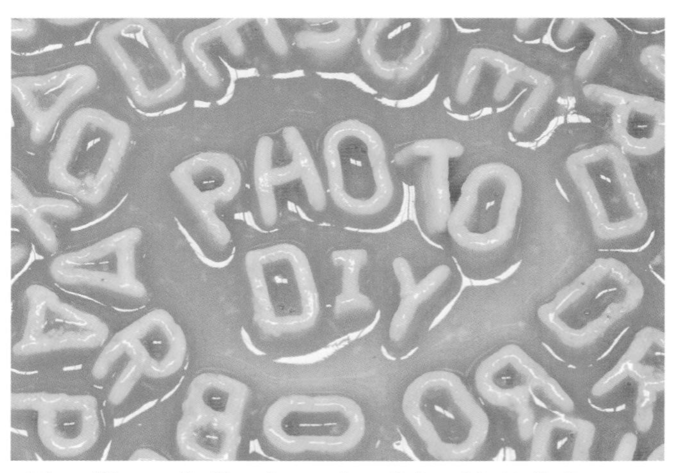

4 I wasn't happy with either of my previous efforts, so I decided to dispense with the spoon – instead of creating interest, it was proving a distraction. This time, I cropped in tighter, filling the frame with the alphabet spaghetti. The window light provided ample lighting and I used a tripod to ensure my picture remained shake-free at an exposure of 1/4sec at f/11.

Final image
I decided the alphabet spaghetti would look better shot in a vertical composition. The format change meant I had to rearrange the surrounding letters, leaving a larger gap around PHOTO DIY.

Make a splash!

ROSS HODDINOTT: Water is highly photogenic, whether in large quantities or a tiny droplet. H_2O seems to be irresistible to photographers: they can 'suspend' it by using a fast shutter speed or render it as a milky blur with a lengthy exposure, capture reflections off its surface or use it to add the feeling of motion to an image. There is an infinite number of ways to shoot it, so it's no wonder that water features in so many of our images.

One picture that many photographers want to take is a close-up of a droplet splashing into water. Yes, it is a bit of a cliché, but done well it creates a very striking image.

You don't need much room; a simple tabletop set-up in your kitchen or living room will suffice. And you only need a basic set-up: a digital camera; close-up filter or macro lens; a single flashgun and a handful of everyday bits and bobs. Within half an hour or so, you can be set up and ready to begin taking beautiful images of sculptured water droplets.

Get ready!

TIME REQUIRED
30 MINUTES

EQUIPMENT USED
NIKON D300, SIGMA 105MM LENS, TRIPOD, REMOTE RELEASE, SPEEDLIGHT SB-800 FLASH & FLASH CORD

ALSO USED
CONTAINER, PLASTIC BAG, PENCIL & TOWEL

Keep everything dry!

It's important to keep your gear dry to prevent damage to electronics. It's worth keeping a towel handy at all times to wipe down your camera body and lens when needed

1 Before you begin taking pictures, you need to arrange your set-up. You will need a container, half to three-quarters full of water, for your droplet to fall into. I used a paint tray but any large, shallow container will do. I placed this on a still-life table, but a simple tabletop set-up would do fine. Next, suspend a bag – partially full of water – 30-60cm directly overhead.

Essential kit

FLASHGUN:
An off-camera flash is required for this technique. You need a flashgun that can be used via a wireless transmitter or TTL flash cord. The flashgun then needs to be positioned so that it illuminates the surface being reflected in the water – in other words, you direct the flash burst at the water droplet's background. Adjust power output and move the flashgun to different positions to alter the final result.

2 I position my tripod-mounted Nikon D300 so it's shooting down into the water tray. Next, it's time to consider lighting. You need to illuminate what you see reflected in the water through the viewfinder – not the water itself. I placed a sheet of white card at the end of the tray to create a simple background and angled my flashgun towards the card.

3 Now the technical bit. It's the pulse of the flashgun that dictates your shutter speed. I rarely use flash myself, but it's fairly straightforward. I set it to its Manual mode and dialled in 1/16th power to generate a fast enough speed to freeze the droplets. This is a good starting point so I recommend you use the same and make adjustments after reviewing results.

Final image

After 30 minutes, I had taken some nice images but they lacked colour, so I altered White Balance from Auto to its Tungsten WB preset. Deliberately mismatching WB in this way gave my final image a blue hue.

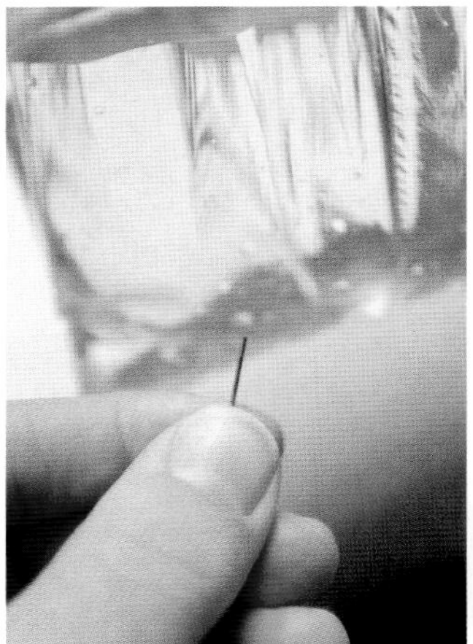

4 I made a tiny hole in the bag using a pin to create a constant drip and held a pencil in the water at the point where the droplets were falling so that I could focus manually. I set an aperture of f/8 to generate enough depth-of-field to keep the droplet sharp but render any ripples attractively out of focus. I set the flash sync speed to 1/200sec and set a low ISO rating of 200 for optimum quality.

5 Time to get started. Good timing and a huge slice of luck are required, so take lots of shots – hundreds possibly – to get what you are after. It is an unpredictable technique and every image is different. Expect lots of 'near misses', such as water ripples but no droplet. I found a remote release helped my timing, releasing the shutter as the droplet hit the water.

Outdoor Indoor Lighting Creative Photoshop

Shoot some smoke trails

SAILESH PATEL: An easy way to create stunning, abstract images with a mystical air is to shoot some smoke trails. I've used incense sticks for this technique as they are relatively safe for indoor use and provide just the right viscosity of smoke for this sort of result. As the smoke always rises in a slightly different way, there's an infinite variety of shapes and patterns to shoot. Once you've captured your smoke trail shots, there's also a wealth of options for adjusting them to create some truly magical results. Each trail can be coloured, flipped, dodged, burned or distorted in post-production to create other shapes. There is literally no limit to the potential of this technique. However, it is important to ensure that the incense sticks are used responsibly, as they can cause fires. Make sure that once they are lit, you stay with them at all times.

Get ready!

TIME REQUIRED
45 MINUTES

EQUIPMENT USED
CANON EOS 10D WITH 100MM MACRO LENS, CANON SPEEDLITE 430EX FLASHGUN, WIRELESS FLASH TRIGGER

ALSO USED
BLACK FABRIC & CARD, INCENSE STICKS, SHEET OF GLASS, STUDIO TABLE

1 I cover a studio table with a black cloth, adding a sheet of glass (a ceramic dish will also suffice) to reduce any risk of fire. I then stick the incense stick to the glass with Blu-Tack. I mount my flashgun behind the incense, with a piece of black card stuck to the far side of it, to prevent the light spilling out onto the background. I set up my camera (and wireless flash trigger) on a tripod, and open windows to ensure that the room is properly ventilated.

2 I set my camera to Manual mode and switch the lens to manual focus, pre-focusing for the area just above the incense. I set a shutter speed of 1/200sec – my camera's fastest flash sync speed – and an aperture of f/14, to give me sufficient depth-of-field. I also set my camera to record the images in Raw format, as this will not only provide the best quality images possible, it will also allow me to enrich the blacks in the conversion process.

3 Once I'm ready to start shooting, I carefully light the incense, making sure that the stick is stuck securely and in no danger of falling onto the black fabric. For comfort's sake, I use a remote release to fire the shutter. Once I have taken between 30 and 40 shots, I make sure that the incense is completely extinguished and then review the images on my LCD screen. I'm mainly looking to check that no light from the flashgun has hit the background.

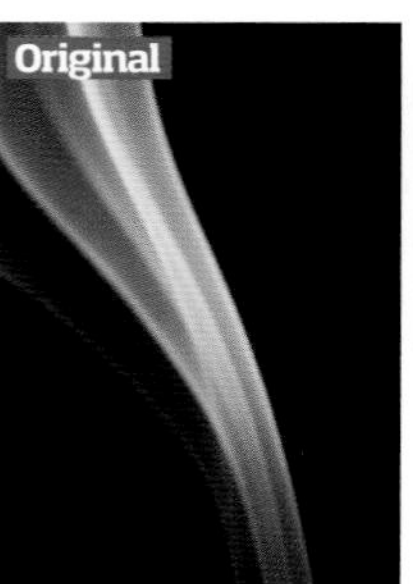

4 Once I am satisfied with the results, I upload the images to my computer. In Adobe's Camera Raw converter, I use the Blacks slider to darken the background before opening the file. I then use the Eraser tool in Photoshop to clean up any unwanted smoke spread. Next, I invert the image (*Image>Adjustments>Invert*). This will change the smoke trails to a hazy black and the background to a crisp, pure white – making the image stand out more.

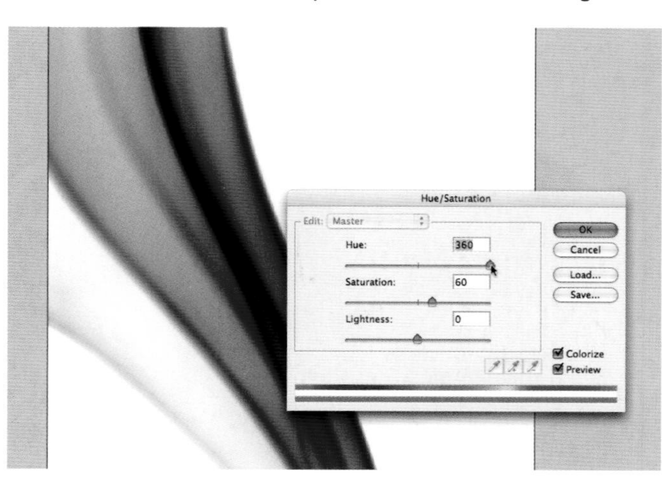

5 To add further interest to the shot and give it real impact, I decide to add some colour. In Photoshop's Hue/Saturation palette, I tick the Colorize and Preview boxes, before moving the sliders around until I'm happy. I choose this rich red colour, and a saturation of 75 per cent. I then save the image under a new file name. Next, I open a different image and repeat steps three and four, but I decide to colour the second smoke trail with a rich blue.

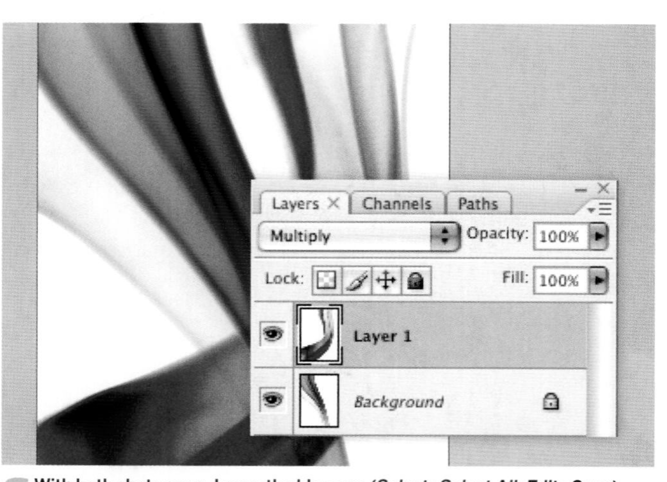

6 With both shots open, I copy the blue one (*Select>Select All; Edit>Copy*) and paste it onto the red image (*Edit>Paste*). I reduce the opacity of the blue image and move it around until it looks good. To align the images, I use the Free Transform tool (*Ctrl+T*). I then return the opacity of the blue layer to 100% and change the Layer Blending Mode from Normal to Multiply. Finally, I flatten the image (*Layer>Flatten Image*) and save as a new file again.

Final image

After a few final tweaks to the Curves, Saturation and Contrast, I'm very happy with my final image. It is a very colourful abstract that could look great as a canvas print on any wall.

Shoot fruit!

STEWART BYWATER: Inspiration for an image can come from anywhere, and I got the idea for this shot when I saw a billboard advertising a particular brand of alcoholic drink. The technique I used is a great one to try, as it allows you to produce a varied series of images, simply by making very minor adjustments. I decided to backlight the fruit to give it a slight glow, and to try and capture the bubbles as they rose to the top, to create a more dynamic image.

Get ready!

TIME REQUIRED
20 MINUTES

EQUIPMENT USED
CANON EOS 10D
100MM F/2.8 MACRO
TRIPOD & REMOTE
STUDIOFLASH LIGHTS

ALSO USED
COFFEE JAR, LEMON & LIME, SPARKLING WATER & ICE CUBES

Outdoor
Indoor
Lighting
Creative
Photoshop

Technique watch

LIGHTING: I used a studio table for my shots, but if you don't have one, any table would work, with a white sheet, or some thick paper placed over it. For the background, a sheet of white card works just fine (though for more unusual results, you could also try coloured backgrounds). I used two Interfit studioflash lights, although any basic studioflash or continuous lighting system is suitable. One light was aimed at the white background, to make sure that it looked white in the shot, rather than a dull grey colour. This would also bounce the light back onto the subject, giving the fruit a translucent glow. The other light was positioned over the jar, to light the subject. I then carefully adjusted the position of the lights and the jar, to minimise the reflections that appeared on the front of the jar.

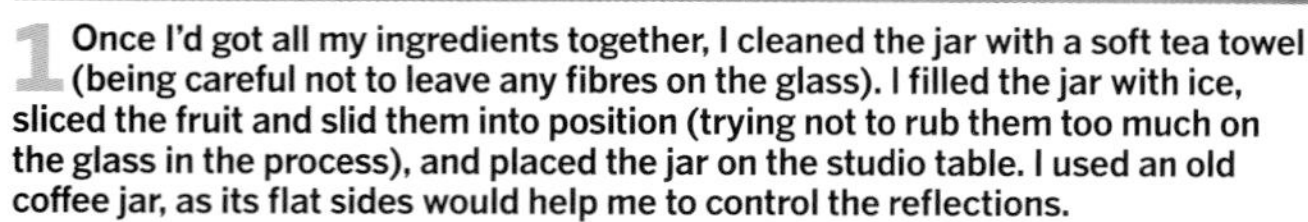

1 Once I'd got all my ingredients together, I cleaned the jar with a soft tea towel (being careful not to leave any fibres on the glass). I filled the jar with ice, sliced the fruit and slid them into position (trying not to rub them too much on the glass in the process), and placed the jar on the studio table. I used an old coffee jar, as its flat sides would help me to control the reflections.

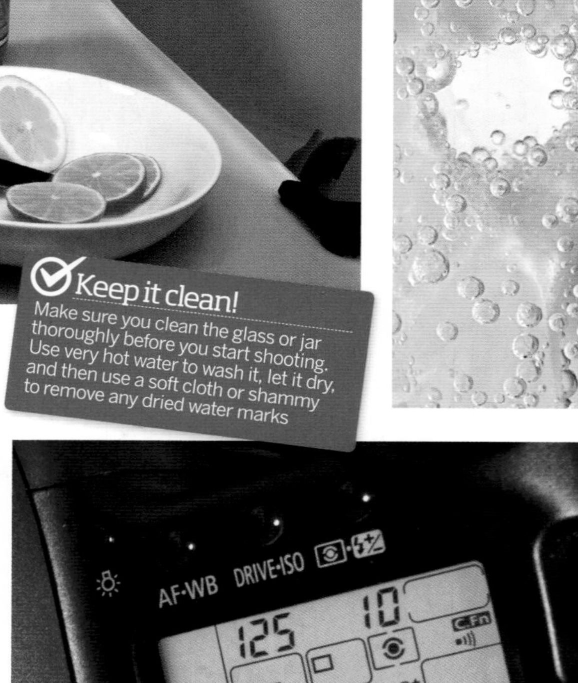

Keep it clean!

Make sure you clean the glass or jar thoroughly before you start shooting. Use very hot water to wash it, let it dry, and then use a soft cloth or shammy to remove any dried water marks

2 I set my camera up on a tripod, attached a remote release and plugged the lights in (I used Pocket Wizards to trigger them, but a sync lead would have worked just as well). I turned the lights on and made sure they were positioned to light the subject nicely, whilst minimising the reflections on the jar. I then checked my focus, and locked it by switching the lens to MF mode.

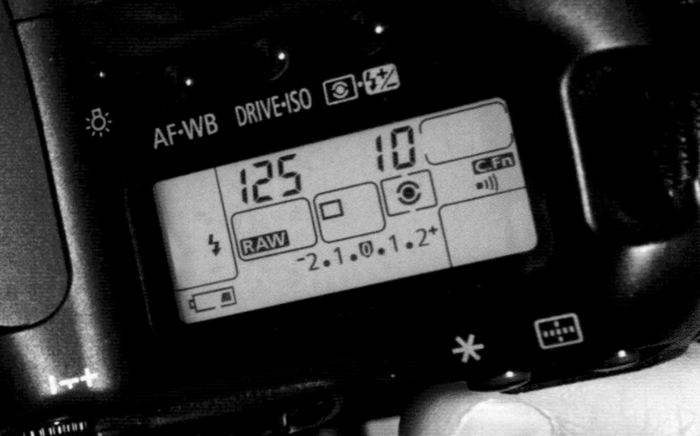

3 I set my camera's White Balance to Flash (set it to Tungsten if you're shooting with lamps), and the exposure mode to Manual. I set the shutter speed to sync at 1/125sec and then took a flash exposure reading and adjusted the power of the light to give me a working aperture of f/10, which would provide sufficient depth-of-field. A test shot confirmed a good exposure.

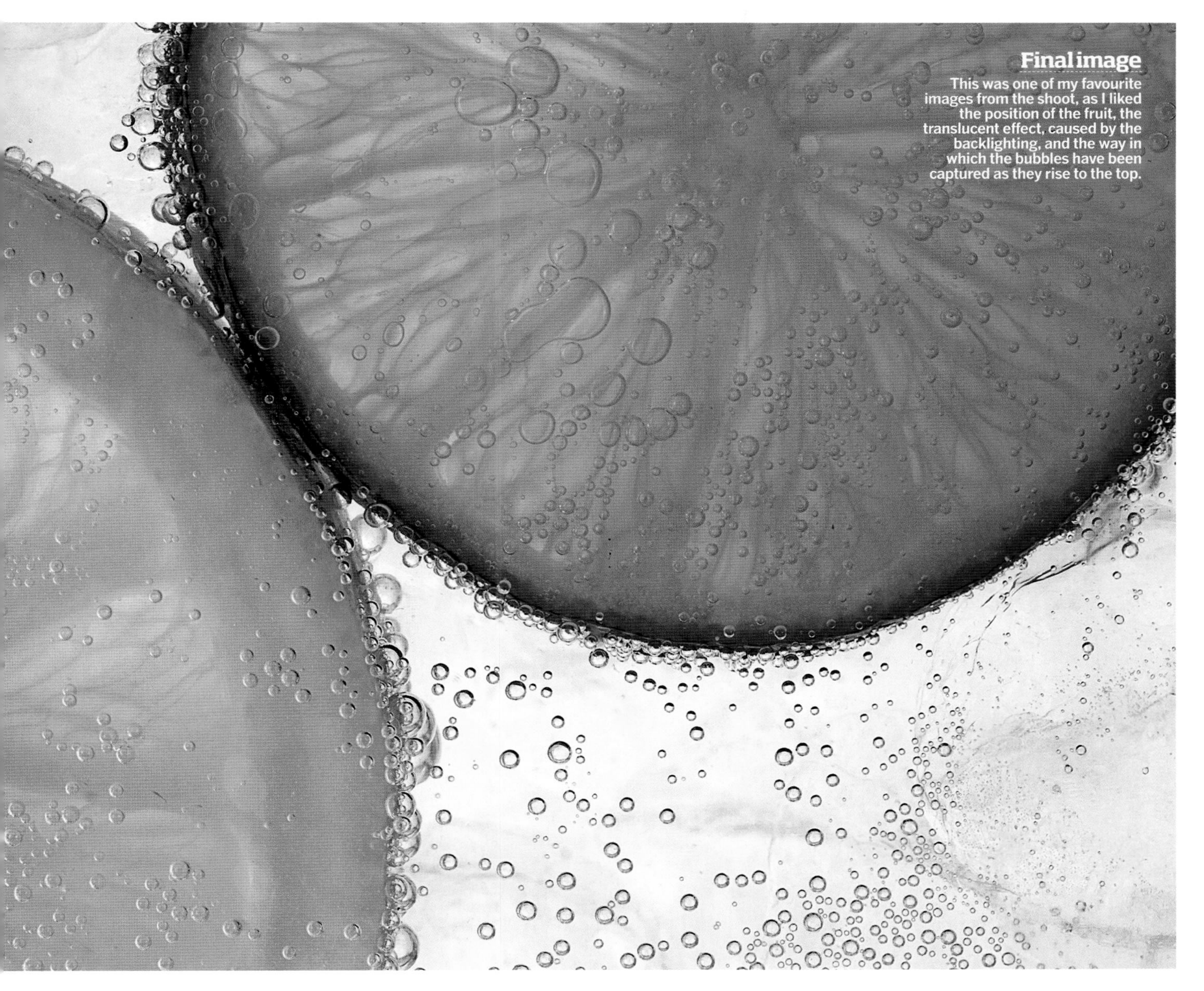

Final image
This was one of my favourite images from the shoot, as I liked the position of the fruit, the translucent effect, caused by the backlighting, and the way in which the bubbles have been captured as they rise to the top.

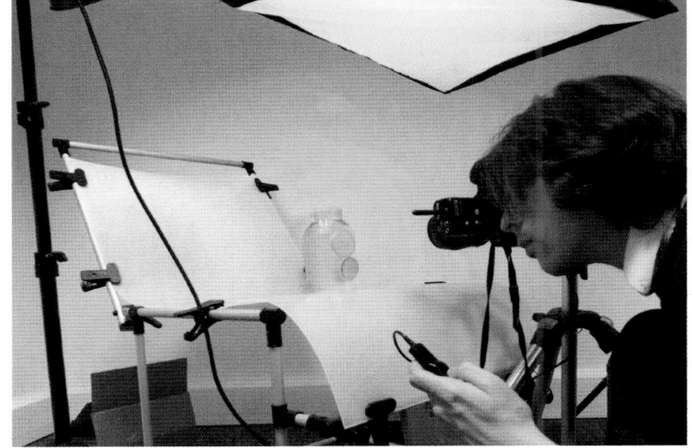

4 The next step was to pour the sparkling water onto the ice. When the jar was nearly full, I took several shots. Once satisfied, I adjusted the composition by moving the tripod slightly. I then refocused and shot a few more frames, to get a good variety of images. Shooting straight after the water was poured gave the best results, as there were more bubbles in the shots.

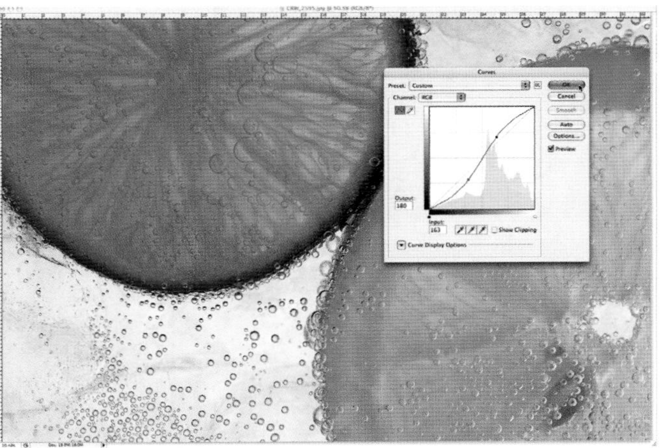

5 The final step was to transfer my images to my computer. In Photoshop, I adjusted the contrast by creating an 'S curve' in the Curves tool. To make the bubbles stand out more, I then applied some Unsharp Mask, adjusting the amounts of sharpness and radius to get the optimal result. I tweaked the Colour Balance slightly as well, to make the colours look 'punchy'.

Outdoor Indoor Lighting Creative Photoshop

Create window-lit fine-art silhouettes

IAN FARRELL: Silhouettes are graphic images that not only look great, but are easy to produce too. All you need is a plain background that's lit more brightly than the subject in front of it. As for what to shoot, some subjects work better than others, so experimentation is key, but it's worth seeking out objects with some transparency or fine detail in them. After some trial and error, I found long grasses to be particularly suitable. They're around all through the summer, and grow in large numbers. The source of your bright background can be as simple or as complicated as you like. If you have studio lighting, a softbox makes a great white background. Alternatively, light a sheet of paper from the rear with a flashgun, or even just tape a piece of tracing or photocopier paper to a window for a simple but effective solution. We used the paper-on-window approach for the photographs you see here. It's such a simple approach that the whole thing was done and dusted in 15 minutes!

Get ready!

TIME REQUIRED
15 MINUTES

EQUIPMENT USED
NIKON D700 & 50MM F/1.4 STANDARD LENS

ALSO USED
SHEET OF WHITE PAPER, GRASSES, THISTLES, DANDELIONS, ETC

SETTING UP: A piece of ordinary A3 copier paper taped to a south-facing window on a sunny day will make a great background for our silhouette image. Tracing paper works well under cloudier conditions. Our subject is then placed in front of the paper.

1 Setting your camera to an auto exposure mode, or metering in manual, straight from the paper, won't give you a good result: a camera's metering aims to make things 18% grey, not white. Instead, start at your meter's indicated exposure in manual mode and take pictures while lengthening the shutter speed, watching the histogram until you can see proper whites at the right-hand side of the graph.

2 With your correct exposure locked in, using Manual mode, bring in your subject, positioning it slightly away from the background. You'll want to use a shallow depth-of-field to render the paper out of focus and, therefore, devoid of any distracting detail. You may be able to hold the grass stem with one hand and your camera with the other, but we'd highly recommend a clamp or vase to make this step much easier!

Technique watch

WATCH YOUR TONE! This type of image is just begging for some toning to really set it off. There are so many ways of doing this. A great option is to use the split-toning feature in Photoshop's CS3's Camera Raw conversion plug-in.

3 **TWEAKING THE RESULT:** Inspect the results of your efforts on your computer – if it's not quite the effect you hoped for, you can tweak things with a simple Levels adjustment. In Adobe Photoshop or Elements, choose *Image>Adjustments>Levels* and pull the right-hand marker inwards to make the background whiter. Then tweak the left-hand marker to deepen the blacks somewhat until you're happy with the effect.

4 **EXTENDING YOUR CANVAS:** Sometimes graphic compositions like this can benefit from some extra white in the composition – known in the trade as 'negative space'. An easy way to do this is with the Crop Tool. Draw around the whole of the canvas with it, then use a drag handle to extend the box beyond the existing image. Hit return and new space will be added and filled with the background colour – which in this case should be white.

Final image

A semi-silhouetted approach works well for this stem of grass. This was achieved by not moving the black point in Photoshop's Levels adjustment screen too much.

Outdoor Indoor Lighting Creative Photoshop

Scan a flower with ease

LEE FROST: Few photographers realise it, but the humble flatbed scanner is not only good at scanning flat artwork – you can also use it as a large-format digital scanning camera, to 'photograph' 3D objects and produce images of astounding quality. Even a budget-priced scanner like the Epson Perfection V500 used here is capable of results way beyond a top-end digital SLR. I've been experimenting with this technique for some time now, scanning natural objects such as flowers, seeds, heads and leaves to create beautiful fine-art images. In this technique I'll show you how it's done, and explain how the original scanned image is just the beginning of a creative adventure.

Get ready!

TIME REQUIRED
1 HOUR

EQUIPMENT USED
EPSON PERFECTION V500 SCANNER

ALSO USED
BOXFILE, GERBERA & PHOTOSHOP CS3

1 The first step is to give the platen (the glass plate) a good clean with a microfibre cloth to remove as much dust as you can. This will reduce the amount of spotting you have to do to clean-up the scan. When you've done that, take your chosen object (flowers, leaves and other natural subjects are ideal) and place it on the platen. Take care not to scratch the platen with sharp objects.

Essential kit

FLATBED SCANNER: Flatbed scanners are often seen as a cheap alternative to a dedicated film scanner. However, while most may not be able to scan film originals as well as a proper film scanner, they're far more versatile for general use and every photographer should own one! The good news is that you won't need to break the bank to buy one. The Epson Perfection V500 is a budget option and boasts a resolution of 6400dpi – which means pin-sharp prints measuring 24x20in or more at 300dpi are easily achievable. The V500 is also the first CCD scanner to use LEDs as a light source so instead of hanging around for ages while it warms up, just one second after flicking the 'On' switch you'll be ready to scan.

2 As the lid of the scanner can't be lowered with the object on the platen, you need to make your own DIY hood to cover it. I used an old box file sprayed inside with matt black paint. By cutting the lid off I was left with a black box 4in deep, which I placed over the object. Not only does it contain the light from the scanner, but it also creates a plain black background.

3 Open your scanner software and create a preview scan of the object. Make any adjustments to contrast, exposure and colour balance, then set the output size of the scan – I chose 16x12in at 300dpi. When you're all done, click on SCAN and sit back and wait for the scanner to do its job – this usually takes a couple of minutes if the output size is reasonably large.

4 When the scanning is complete, open the image in Photoshop and enlarge it to 100%. Not only does this show just how impressive the image quality is, but it will also highlight any dust spots and blemishes that can be removed using the Healing Brush Tool or Clone Stamp Tool.

5 Once the image is 'clean', it's time to put your imagination and creativity to good use. Make a copy so you've an unaltered original and then try things like boosting contrast, converting it to black & white, toning it or adding filter effects such a Diffuse Glow or some Gaussian Blur.

6 For the image shown in this step-by-step, I converted the original colour scan to black & white using *Image>Adjustments>Black & White* in Photoshop CS3 then experimented with Levels and Curves before adding Diffuse Glow and Gaussian Blur to an adjustment layer. Easy!

Final image
A beautiful image of a flower captured without the use of a camera. Isn't the digital age amazing!

Try adding a texture!
Add extra interest to your scan images by scanning a sheet of greaseproof paper to create a texture screen, then combine it with the main image and adjust the opacity of the texture screen layer until you're happy with the effect

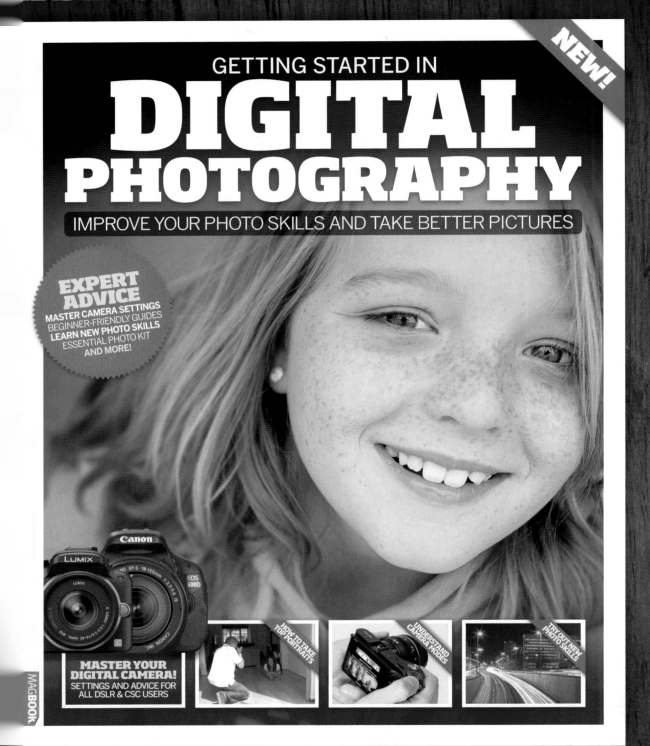

Step-by-step tutorials

LIGHTING PROJECTS

SWITCH ON YOUR FLASHGUN, STUDIOFLASH OR YOUR FLASHLIGHT FOR IMAGINATIVE RESULTS

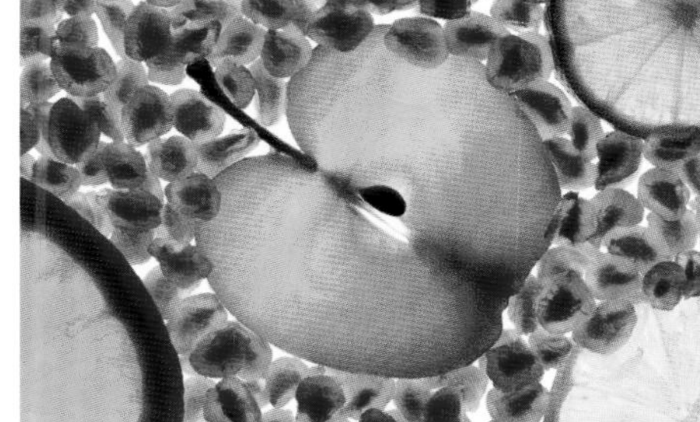

Give it a swirl!

HELEN SOTIRIADIS: Capturing light trails is usually an outdoor, night-time activity but it's just as much fun trying indoors, and also often far more achievable. All you need is a dark room in your home and a strong LED torch for painting shapes and to illuminate the prop, which is being added to improve the composition. Most people try this technique without objects and just spell words or draw a simple shape, such as a heart or star in the air, but having something to draw patterns around – especially if it's reflective like a glass – can make the image look less humdrum and much more impressive.

Get ready!

TIME REQUIRED
45 MINUTES

EQUIPMENT USED
CANON EOS 40D
WITH CANON EF 50MM
F/1.4 LENS

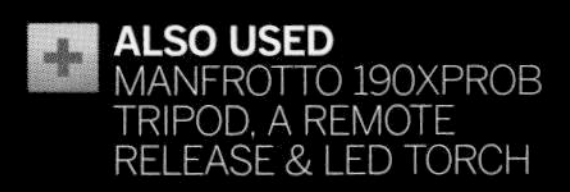

ALSO USED
MANFROTTO 190XPROB
TRIPOD, A REMOTE
RELEASE & LED TORCH

Essential kit

WHICH LED TORCH?
Finding the right LED torch for this technique can be tricky; too large and your light trails could merge together, too small and you could struggle illuminating the prop. Try to find one that's compact and lightweight so it's easy to manoeuvre and gives off a strong, highly-defined light beam. Ideally opt for one with multiple bulbs (the torch used here has nine) as it will provide more interesting swirls, enriching a potentially bland composition. The colour of the light is also worth considering, too.

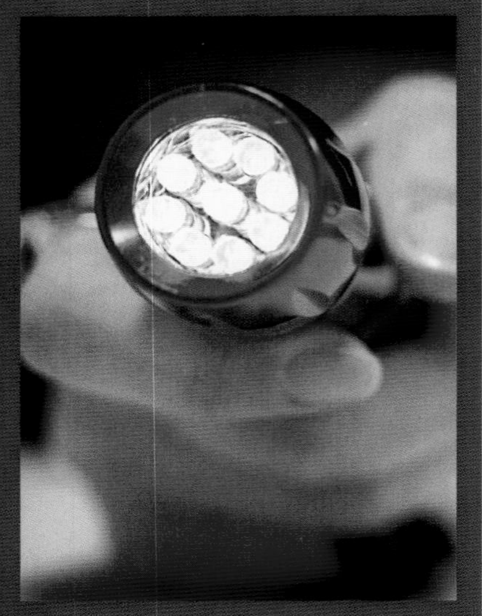

Final image

This shot required very little post-production. I created an exposure adjustment layer in Photoshop (*Layer>New Adjustment Layer>Exposure*), increasing gamma to darken any hints of light on the black background and base. Finally, I used the Healing Brush Tool to clean up bits of stray dust on the reflective surface and the glass itself.

1 I used a water-filled fluted glass for this shot to create refractions of light. As the light accentuates fingerprints and dust, make sure the glass is clean, and after filling it, wipe the outside and the inside above the water level to avoid stray droplets. I used a very strong LED torch, with a cool blue light, but to be more creative cover the torch with coloured cellophane.

2 The set-up for this image is simple and costs almost nothing. Bend a large sheet of black construction paper so it leans against a cardboard box, steadied by the weight of a few books. I used a sheet of dark, tinted glass but you could use a second piece of card as a base. The camera must be completely still for the duration of the shot, so mount it onto a tripod.

3 While the room is still lit, compose the scene and focus on the glass. If you used autofocus rather than manual focus, turn it off before you switch the lights off or the camera will try unsuccessfully to refocus in the dark. Set the camera to manual mode to allow you to vary the shutter speed and set the aperture to f/22. Turn off the lights and start shooting!

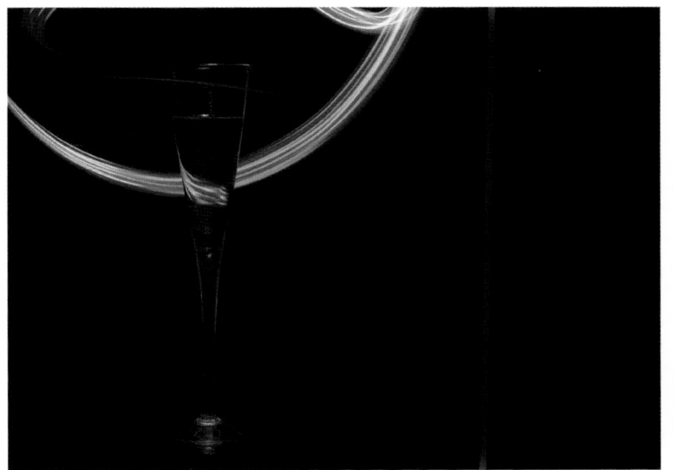

4 Remember to spend a few seconds shining light on the side of the prop to illuminate it and to think about the types of shapes you want to create. My first few attempts were too high, too sparse or too low (creating an undesirable reflection in the base) or just the wrong shape. It took a few attempts, but finally I started getting results I was pleased with.

5 Initially, I used a five-second exposure but I didn't have enough time to illuminate the glass from the side with the torch and create enough light trails. This technique is all about trial and error, so try different shapes and prolong the shutter speed. I found ten seconds was ideal as it allowed plenty of time to light the glass and to create pleasing swirls.

Outdoor Indoor Lighting Creative Photoshop

Add colour with flash gels

DANIEL LEZANO: Getting to use just one flashgun proves a daunting prospect for many, so how does the thought of using two grab you? This technique deals with showing you how to light a subject with one flashgun, while a second flash is used to illuminate the background. This technique is useful when you want to highlight detail in the scene or, as shown here, you want to use flash gels to light it in a completely different colour. While this may sound difficult, it's actually quite easy to achieve. You need to use your camera's integral flash (or a hotshoe-mounted flashgun) to illuminate your subject, which is pretty straightforward as the exposure is taken care of automatically by the camera thanks to the wonders of TTL flash. A second flashgun is triggered automatically by the main flash to illuminate the background, so you've little to do other than ensure that the remote flash is set up correctly, which as the panel on the right reveals, is pretty easy to do.

Flash gels are small sheets of coloured plastic that are placed over the flash head to colour the flash output. The flash gel is held in place over the head via Velcro or an elastic band and with a number of kits available with a choice of colours, it's an inexpensive and easy way to add creative flash effects to your images. Larger flash gel kits are available for studioflash heads too, so the technique used here can easily be applied to studioflash set-ups as well as flashguns.

Using flash gels to illuminate a background is equally suited to both indoor and outdoor locations. Plain backdrops as well as textured surfaces are suitable, although the latter does provide additional visual interest. It's also worth bearing in mind that you can use more than one flashgun for the background, so feel free to mix colour gels.

Get ready!

TIME REQUIRED
30 MINUTES

EQUIPMENT USED
CANON EOS 500D & SPEEDLITE 580EX

ALSO USED
COLOURED GELS

1 Here's our subject photographed using only our hotshoe-mounted flashgun. She's well exposed but the background is drab and dark.

2 We've set up a remote flashgun behind her, which fires to light the wall in the background but the effect isn't particularly attractive.

Remote flashgun set-up

WAYS TO TRIGGER A REMOTE FLASHGUN: Depending on the types of flashgun and accessories you are using, there are a number of ways of triggering your remote 'gelled' flash. If you have a dedicated flashgun with a slave function, you can use the Master/ Slave facility to trigger it when you release the shutter. You'll need to refer to your camera/flashgun instructions as this varies according to the camera/flash brand and mode. Alternatively, you can fit a slave cell to the bottom of any flashgun, which is then triggered by the output from the camera's built-in or hotshoe-mounted flashgun (depending on which you are using).

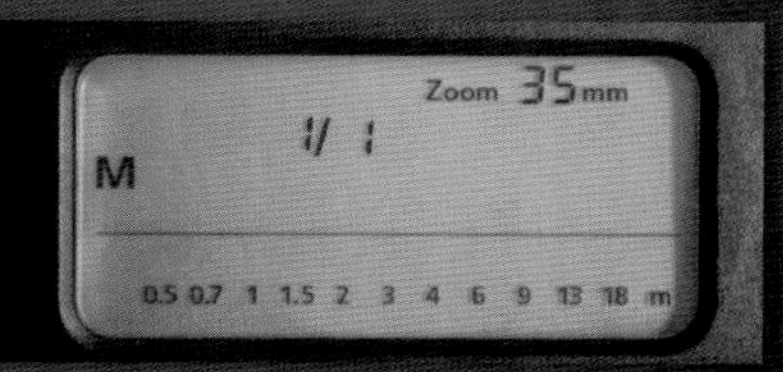

SETTING UP THE EXPOSURE ON THE REMOTE FLASHGUN: If you're using a dedicated Master/Slave flash system to trigger the off-camera flashgun, then you can either set up its output to be based on a TTL exposure or manual power setting. While selecting TTL is normally the best choice, we'd actually recommend you set the flash to manual for this technique, as the results will be more consistent. If you are using a slave flash, you should set the flashgun to manual to allow you to set a specific power setting. With the flash in manual, you can set the remote flash to fire at fixed power settings such as full power (1/1), half power (1/2), quarter power (1/4) and so on. Take some test shots and adjust the power settings to suit the scene. Adjust power if you want a stronger or weaker effect or if you switch colour gels, as some absorb more light than others.

3 We've fitted a Lumiquest red gel and the colour adds interest, but, with the remote flash set to TTL, its output isn't as strong as we'd like.

4 Setting the remote flash to manual power provides a far stronger output, although the full-power (1/1) setting is far too strong.

5 We try various manual power settings to see which provides the best result and find that for the half-power setting works best.

Final image
While the red gel is attractive, it proves overpowering, so we try various colours and find green works the best.

Turn your little angel into a devil

STEWART BYWATER: A technique that I've wanted to try for quite a long time is to take a photograph where the subject's shadow appears to be different from the subject that has cast it. I've seen this done a number of times, and often wondered how it was executed. There are several ways in which it could be done, most involving very clever lighting techniques and an understanding of scale and trajectory. This seemed somewhat over-complicated, so I tried to think of a simpler way of doing it. In the end, I decided to shoot two exposures using a white paper studio backdrop, with one light placed in front of it and one light behind. For the 'shadow' exposure I would place the subject behind the paper, as it was thin enough to let his shadow show through, yet thick enough so that it would not be completely transparent. For the portrait image, I placed him in front of the paper. I would later merge the two in Photoshop. However, it's worth pointing out that if you had two people of roughly the same build, who would project a similar silhouette, you could get the result with a single shot.

Get ready!

TIME REQUIRED
ONE HOUR

EQUIPMENT
CANON EOS 10D WITH 17-40MM LENS, TWO INTERFIT STUDIOFLASH HEADS, POCKETWIZARDS, LASTOLITE WHITE STUDIO BACKGROUND PAPER ROLL

ALSO USED
DEVIL PROPS & WINDMILL

SETTING UP: Small children can get bored very quickly if they're just standing around waiting, so I decided to practise this technique before my subject arrived. I placed one studio light behind the white paper background, pointing roughly at where I wanted the 'devil' shadow to appear. I then set a stool between the two for the subject to stand on. I placed a second studioflash head – this time with a softbox attached – off to the side where I wanted the 'angel' to stand. I then asked two colleagues to stand in place and took a series of test shots until I was happy with my exposure. The backlight was on full power, while the light at the front, fitted with a softbox, was set to around 1/3 power. Next, I switched my DSLR to manual exposure mode, setting the shutter to its maximum flash sync speed of 1/60sec and an aperture of f/22.

Essential kit

STUDIOFLASH LIGHTS
While this technique could be achieved without studioflash, they do make it a lot easier. The main reason for this is that you can adjust each light's power to find the perfect balance between the foreground subject and back-light. The lights can also be easily moved into various positions until you get the best results. Studioflash is also a great option in situations where subjects, such as children, might move around a lot, as with many newer DSLRs, they can sync up to 1/250sec, allowing users to capture their subjects sharply.

1 Once my subject had arrived, I showed him my test shots, so that he would understand what we were trying to achieve. I then got him to stand in position, and asked his father to stand in the 'devil' position behind the screen. This would help me with my composition, and also make the 'angel' easier to cut out in Photoshop later. I then took some shots of the 'angel' from various heights and reviewed them on my camera.

2 Having captured a good shot of the child smiling, I asked him to put on the devil horns and hold the trident, and to stand on the chair behind the paper background. His mother was also there to make sure he didn't fall or injure himself. I checked the first shot on my camera's LCD screen, and made sure that everything was exactly right, such as the angle of the windmill/trident and the position of his hands, etc. I then took the 'devil' shot.

Final image

This shot can be done in-camera. But if you're lucky enough to have almost identical subjects to hand, you'd be better off combining two shots. Either way, it's great fun and will leave you with a really fun image.

3 Once I had the necessary images, I transferred them to my computer. After spending a short time selecting two ideal frames – one of the shadow, the other of the subject – I opened them both up in Photoshop. I then used Image>Adjustments>Levels (Ctrl+L) and moved the white slider to the left until the background was almost pure white. Then, using the Magic Wand, I set the Tolerance to ten (pixels) and clicked on the white background to make a selection. I then use Select>Inverse to select the subject.

4 Using Edit>Copy (Ctrl+C) I made a copy of the subject selection and then closed the file and moved onto the shadow image. I used Levels here as I did on the other image to achieve a clear white background, then, using Edit>Paste (Ctrl+V) I placed the copied selection onto the shadow shot. You can move the subject by holding the Ctrl key and moving the mouse and, using Edit>Free Transform (Ctrl+T), resize the subject by dragging any of the corner points while holding the Shift key to ensure scaling is proportional.

Outdoor Indoor Lighting Creative Photoshop

Home studio self-portrait

CAROLINE WILKINSON: Studio photography can be an expensive, and daunting, area of photography to test drive, but often the simplest set-ups prove to be the best. Here, I'll show you how to create an attractive hair light using a table lamp, but you can also use wireless flashguns or a studioflash kit.

A hair light is a flattering technique for portraits, created by a strong directional light behind the subject's head, which produces a soft luminous highlight around the hair. If your subject has short hair, directing the light source at the middle of the head can create a subtle halo effect. Whereas, for subjects with long or curly hair, a more dramatic effect can be achieved by positioning the light at the base of the head so it diffuses through more of the hair. It's also worth experimenting with the position of the main light, in this case a second table lamp, to control where the shadows fall on the face. A reflector will also help with this.

I chose to do this technique as a self-portrait. Unfortunately the one person most photographers shoot the least is themselves, but self-portraits are an ideal way to test lighting and creative techniques. Plus it's easier than you might think!

Get ready!

TIME REQUIRED
60 MINUTES

EQUIPMENT NEEDED
NIKON D300, 50MM LENS & MANFROTTO 055B TRIPOD

ALSO USED
TWO HOUSEHOLD LAMPS & A HANDHELD DIFFUSER

Essential kit: Diffuser

In the same way a reflector can fill in shadows or add warmth to a subject's face, a diffuser can soften the strong effects of artificial light – producing a more flattering result. Whether you can get your hands on a diffuser, or an equally effective alternative, such as grease-proof paper, it's worth bearing in mind that not only will it reduce the amount of light that reaches the camera, but will often alter the White Balance too. Normally this won't pose a problem if you're shooting in Raw, as the colour temperature can be easily reset once you have the images on your computer, but if not the White Balance needs to be changed in-camera to compensate for the lighting conditions.

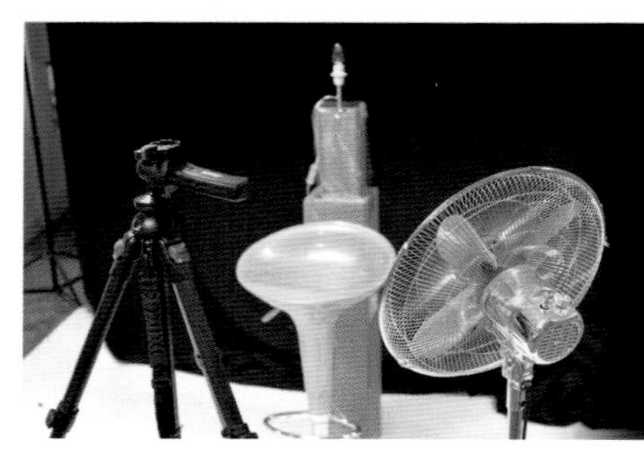

SET-UP: I decided to use a black backdrop for this shot to make the effect of the hair light stand out as much as possible. I positioned my main light source, a tungsten desk lamp, off to the side and high up. If this light is too harsh, consider using a diffuser (or a homemade equivalent) to soften it.

1 HAIR LIGHT I set a standard table lamp, without its shade, between the backdrop and the stool – ensuring the light was directly behind my head and far enough away from the backdrop so not to illuminate it. For optimum highlights, make sure the bulb is level with your head. Use a fan, or have a friend flap a magazine, to lift the hair and add drama to the image.

2 EXPOSURE Although I was shooting a head and shoulders portrait, I framed it so there was plenty of room to crop later in Photoshop. I then set the camera to aperture-priority mode at f/2.8 to get a shallow depth-of-field. Having a large mirror placed beside the camera may help you to gauge how the composition looks before it's taken, but I took a few test shots first to assess the framing and focusing.

3 WHITE BALANCE Although a diffuser can bathe a subject in softer, more flattering light, it can also alter the colour temperature. As I shot in Raw, the White Balance can be easily changed later in Photoshop's Adobe Camera Raw. I therefore took a photo of me holding a white piece of paper, which I could later use to set the White Balance on my computer.

4 INTERVAL SETTING The interval timer is a hidden gem on the Nikon D300. I used it instead of the self-timer as it allowed me to shoot continuous frames at set intervals. A remote trigger would have similar benefits, but the interval timer also adjusts the exposure, focus and metering before each shot. There is a lot of trial and error involved in this technique, so be patient and take lots of shots.

Final image
Using the fan added much needed interest to the image. I left the colours as they were as I liked how the warmth of the glow complemented the soft lighting and shallow depth-of-field. However, for a different look you could try converting it to mono.

Outdoor | Indoor | Lighting | Creative | Photoshop

Bright and beautiful portraits

PAUL WARD: High-key portraits refer to shots leaning heavily towards the highlights, limiting any shadows, for a bright, light-looking portrait. It's a popular technique, adopted by many high-street studios, possibly because it's so easy to shoot and, if needed, to post-process, to get polished, professional-looking results. As a minimum, use two light sources; one to illuminate the subject's face and another to overexpose the background. A home budget studio kit is perfect but, although it's a little trickier, you could try standing your subject in front of a sun-drenched window and illuminating the face with a flashgun. However, luckily, the price of studioflash has tumbled in recent years and it's now possible to buy a studioflash kit (with two flashes, brolly and softbox) for under £200 if you shop around. I used the Jessops Portaflash kit for these shots. It's also important to get the backdrop right: although it's preferable to use a flat, white surface like a wall or a white roll of background paper, you can also get by using just a white bedsheet as long as it's pulled tight to reduce any shadows caused by wrinkles or creases.

Get ready!

TIME REQUIRED
45 MINUTES

EQUIPMENT USED
70-200MM LENS, JESSOPS PORTAFLASH KIT & SILVER REFLECTOR

1 My first job was to arrange the lights around my model, Sophie. I used one studioflash and softbox to light the white wall. By overexposing the background, it prevents the light illuminating the subject from creating shadows on the wall. My second head, fitted with a brolly, was placed to the front right of Sophie. Finally, I rested a reflector on her knees to bounce light under her chin.

2 You'll need to fire off a couple of test shots to fine-tune your settings. I opted to start with an exposure of 1/125sec at f/11 (ISO 200), but my first attempt is a tad on the dark side, losing that bright high-key effect. This is due to slight underexposure, which I can correct by using a wider aperture.

3 I look again at my settings and select an aperture of f/8. Unfortunately, this time the image is too bright and the model's face has burnt out in places, leading to unsightly white areas on her skin. I may be able to rescue some of the detail in Photoshop, but areas that are too white are beyond repair.

Essential kit

REFLECTOR:
As well as the studioflash kit, I also made use of a large reflector. If you don't have a reflector to hand, you can improvise by using a roll of tin foil, or if you're really stuck, a large mirror. That said, reflectors are so cheap now that you can pick one up for less than £20. Choose one that comes with a silver finish, or better still, one with a silver and gold reversible sleeve for extra lighting options.

4 With a new aperture of f/9, I've finally got the correct settings, but this time the reflector has slipped and failed to bounce the light in the right direction. You can see from this image what a difference the reflector makes.

5 With the reflector correctly placed and the camera settings spot on, I'm at last happy with my lighting. While everything is working well, I ask Sophie to try out some different poses and angles and capture a number of shots.

6 Once I've uploaded the correctly exposed image to my computer, I use the Levels slider to increase the brightness of the skin tone. Lastly, I adjust the Saturation slider to decrease the colour slightly before saving my file.

Final image
In under an hour you can produce a quality, high-key shot that brings striking impact to your portraits.

Look at fruit salad with fresh eyes!

ROSS HODDINOTT: Our homes are full of potential pictures, you just need to look at everyday objects with a fresh, creative eye. Small objects are the easiest to illuminate creatively, allowing you plenty of control over the type of lighting – natural or artificial – and also its direction. One of my favourite forms of light is backlighting. Translucent subjects, like coloured plastics, glass and leaves look particularly attractive and eye-catching when backlit. The easiest way to create this type of lighting indoors is to use a lightbox. Many digital converts will already have one from their days of viewing slides. However, if you don't own one, they are relatively cheap to buy or make. All you have to do now is find a suitable subject to shoot. Food is a particularly good still-life subject, especially fruit, with its bright colours and variety of textures. I was making the family a fruit salad one evening when inspiration struck.

Get ready!

TIME TAKEN
45 MINUTES

EQUIPMENT USED
NIKON D700, SIGMA 150MM MACRO LENS & TRIPOD

ALSO USED
LIGHTBOX & VARIOUS TYPES OF FRUITS

1 I returned from the local grocers with an assortment of fruit including apples, pears, an orange, a lemon and a lime, grapes and a pomegranate. I wanted to highlight their shape and form, therefore I carefully cut each one into thin slices to create a photogenic, translucent cross-section of each fruit, ready to arrange on my lightbox.

Technique watch

OPTIMISE DEPTH-OF-FIELD: When you're taking close-ups from overhead, optimise depth-of-field by keeping the camera's sensor plane – marked on the camera body – parallel to the subject. By doing so, you will keep all objects of similar height in focus. If the camera is at an angle to the subject, areas of it will drift out-of-focus, spoiling the crisp, fresh look of the fruit and lessening the impact of the shot.

Essential kit

LIGHTBOX: Backlighting small translucent objects indoors is easy with the help of a lightbox. They are available in a variety of sizes, but A4 size or larger is probably the most versatile and useful. The lightbox can be placed on a tabletop or on the floor, then, with the help of a tripod, position your camera overhead. A lightbox can also create striking silhouettes of small, solid objects.

2 I placed slices of apple, pear and grape on the lightbox. I took time to arrange them so they created a pleasing composition. I tried to fill the image space with the fruit, avoiding large empty spaces that might prove distracting. When happy, I took my first shot. However, backlighting can often fool TTL metering into slight underexposure and the image is too dark.

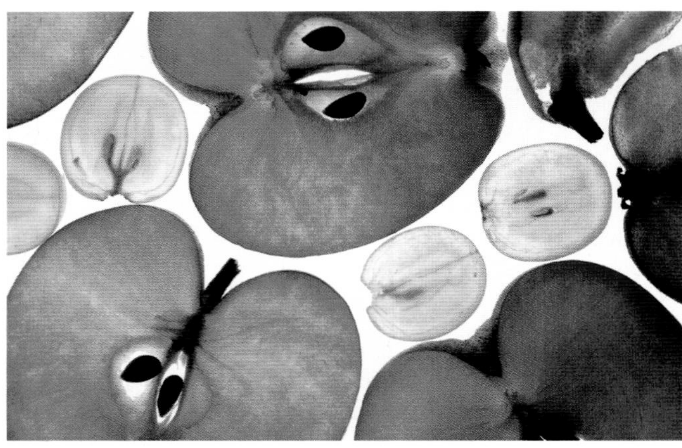

3 I checked the histogram, which confirmed the photo was underexposed, so I applied positive (+) exposure compensation of 2/3EV. This remedied the problem and the subsequent image was exposed correctly. However, the image lacks colour and impact. This type of shot evolves as you go along. Experimentation is the key, so I decided to try some different fruits.

4 In order to add some needed colour, I switched to citrus fruits, using a slice each of orange, lemon and lime. I liked the contrasting colours and sizes of the fruit. I arranged them so that their edges met and the backlighting really emphasised their form and transparency. However, the white gaps between the fruit were distracting and didn't make the best composition, so I decided I needed to fill the entire frame with colour.

5 I scooped out the insides of some kiwi fruit and then carefully placed the juicy results around my fruit slices. I decided to make a slice of apple my key focal point, as this had the most interesting and recognisable outline. I used the slices of citrus fruit to balance the composition. However, I felt I needed to add a splash of red to contrast with the greens and yellows that dominated the image for extra punch.

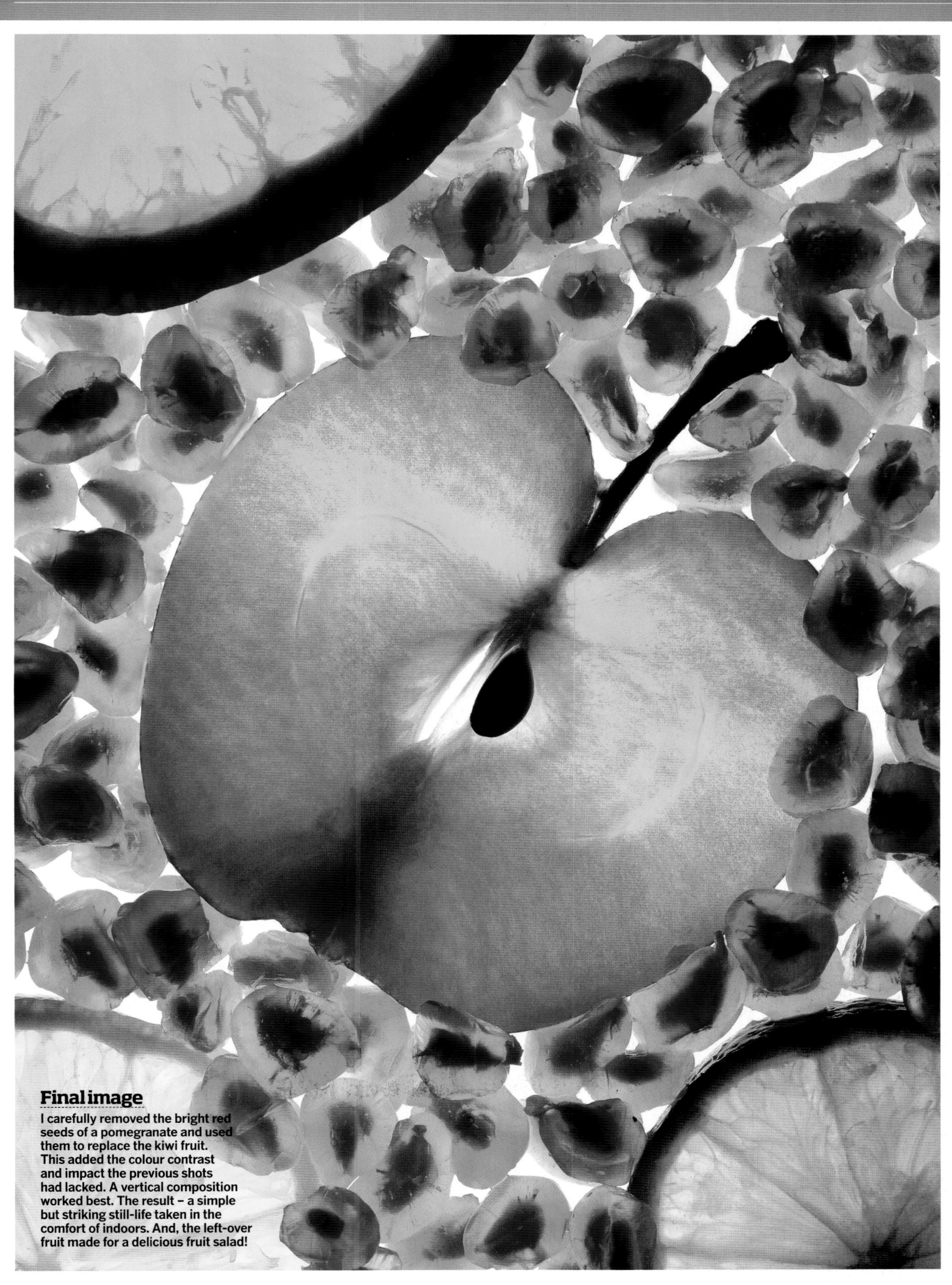

Final image

I carefully removed the bright red seeds of a pomegranate and used them to replace the kiwi fruit. This added the colour contrast and impact the previous shots had lacked. A vertical composition worked best. The result – a simple but striking still-life taken in the comfort of indoors. And, the left-over fruit made for a delicious fruit salad!

Paint a subject with torchlight

DANIEL LEZANO: Painting by light involves using a long exposure and illuminating your subject with a torch (or any other light source for that matter). It's a simple technique that can be used to light a variety of subjects, but works particularly well with still-lifes. The idea is that you must shoot the subject in complete darkness, so that the only light that illuminates your subject comes from the torch. For this step-by-step, a bowl of apples was used to illustrate the technique. The key thing is preparation – set up your equipment correctly and you'll quickly master this technique. As you can see from the shots below, you only need minimal kit to give it a go, so it's something that you should be able to try when you next have a bit of spare time in the evening. One useful bit of advice – set up near a light switch so you don't have to move around too much in the dark!

Get ready!

TIME REQUIRED
20 MINUTES

EQUIPMENT NEEDED
NIKON D60 WITH 18-55MM LENS
MANFROTTO 190X TRIPOD & TORCH

ALSO USED
FRUIT & BOWL

Technique watch

PAINTING WITH LIGHT
So how exactly do you paint with light? It's pretty simple really. During the exposure you simply bathe your subject with light, moving the beam around at different angles and speeds. If you hold the beam over a certain area for a prolonged period, it will appear lighter than areas with minimal exposure, while changing the angle also creates different effects. It's all about trial and error, and every image is different, but it's good fun and produces great results.

Essential kit

TRIPOD: A tripod is an absolutely essential accessory, as you'll be taking long exposures, running into seconds. Any tripod that offers a stable platform is suitable, but if you want to have your camera pointing downwards, as I had, one with a centre column that an be positioned horizontally is ideal. I used the Manfrotto 190XProB, which features an ingenious centre column that can be switched from vertical to horizontal without having to remove it. Any modest digital camera kit is suitable – I used a Nikon D60 with an 18-55mm lens.

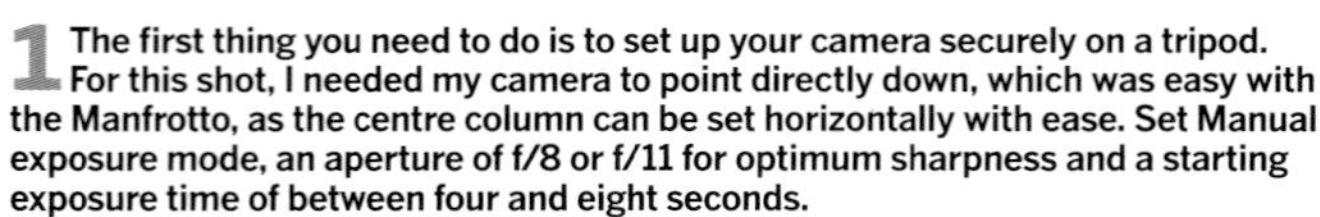

1 The first thing you need to do is to set up your camera securely on a tripod. For this shot, I needed my camera to point directly down, which was easy with the Manfrotto, as the centre column can be set horizontally with ease. Set Manual exposure mode, an aperture of f/8 or f/11 for optimum sharpness and a starting exposure time of between four and eight seconds.

2 Compose the image using the viewfinder (or LiveView) and focus on the subject. Once you've focused, switch the lens from AF to manual focus, because when you switch off the room lights, your camera won't be able to focus in the dark. So long as you don't zoom the lens or move the camera (or subject), the image should stay correctly focused – but check this regularly!

Final image

This was my favourite from the 20 or so images I shot. Very little Photoshop work was needed, other than to crop the image into a square format and to adjust the Levels slightly.

3 Switch off the room light and get into position. Press the shutter button and move the torch in random directions and angles to paint your subject with light. Once the exposure has ended, check the preview and adjust the exposure by changing the shutter speed in full stops (i.e. halve or double it) depending on whether the image is too dark or light for your liking.

4 By changing the angles from which you light the subject, and the amount of time you spend lighting different areas, you'll be able to produce very different results. Experiment with fast random torch movements or more controlled paths of light. You'll also find that a normal torch gives a warm, orange cast, while an LED torch gives a brighter and whiter effect, so try both!

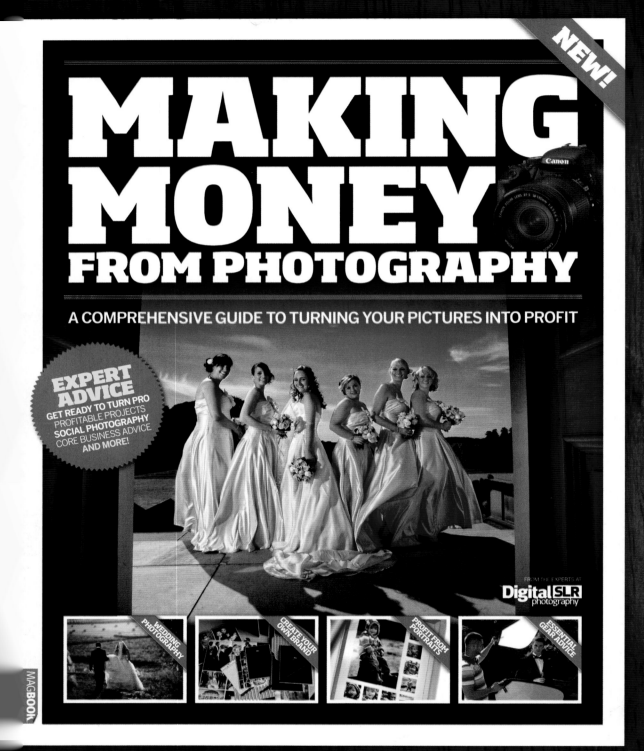

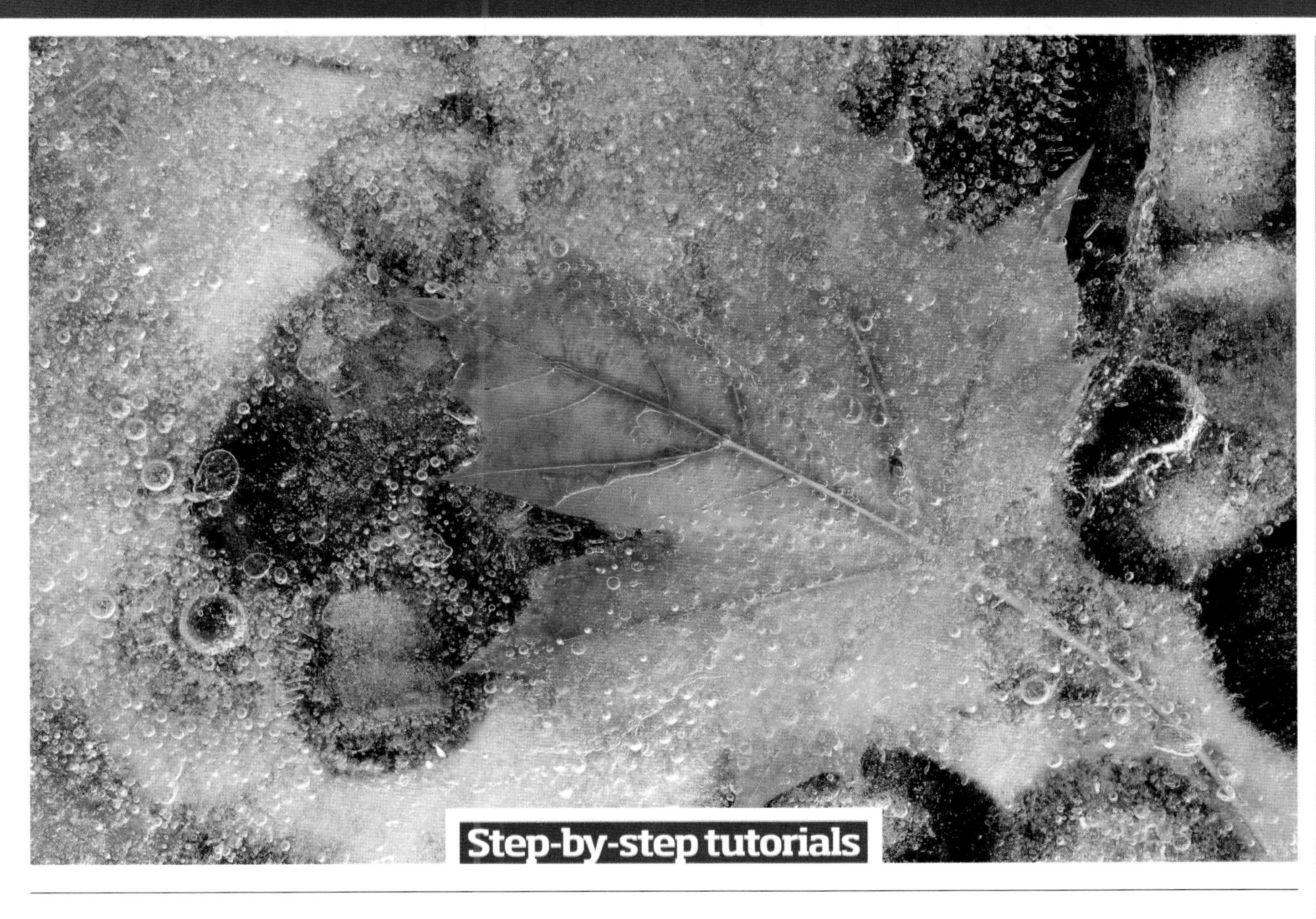

Step-by-step tutorials

CREATIVE PROJECTS

IMPROVE YOUR PHOTO SKILLS WHILE CAPTURING INVENTIVE AND IMAGINATIVE IMAGES

Create a wintery close-up

ROSS HODDINOTT: Our winters are growing increasingly mild, making it more and more difficult to capture great wintery images. Even when there is a hard frost, there is no guarantee you will be able to capture the glistening winter wonderland outside, as you may be working or doing the school run. However, rather than getting frustrated at the lack of opportunities to shoot close-ups of frost and ice, why not create your own by freezing objects in your fridge-freezer. You could freeze practically anything, but feathers and leaves work particularly well. Other than your camera set-up, all you need is your chosen subject, a large (freezable) Pyrex dish, some water, a few spare minutes and a little creativity…

Get ready!

TIME REQUIRED
30 MINUTES

EQUIPMENT USED
NIKON D300 WITH SIGMA 150MM MACRO
TRIPOD & REMOTE

ALSO USED
PRE-FROZEN LEAF

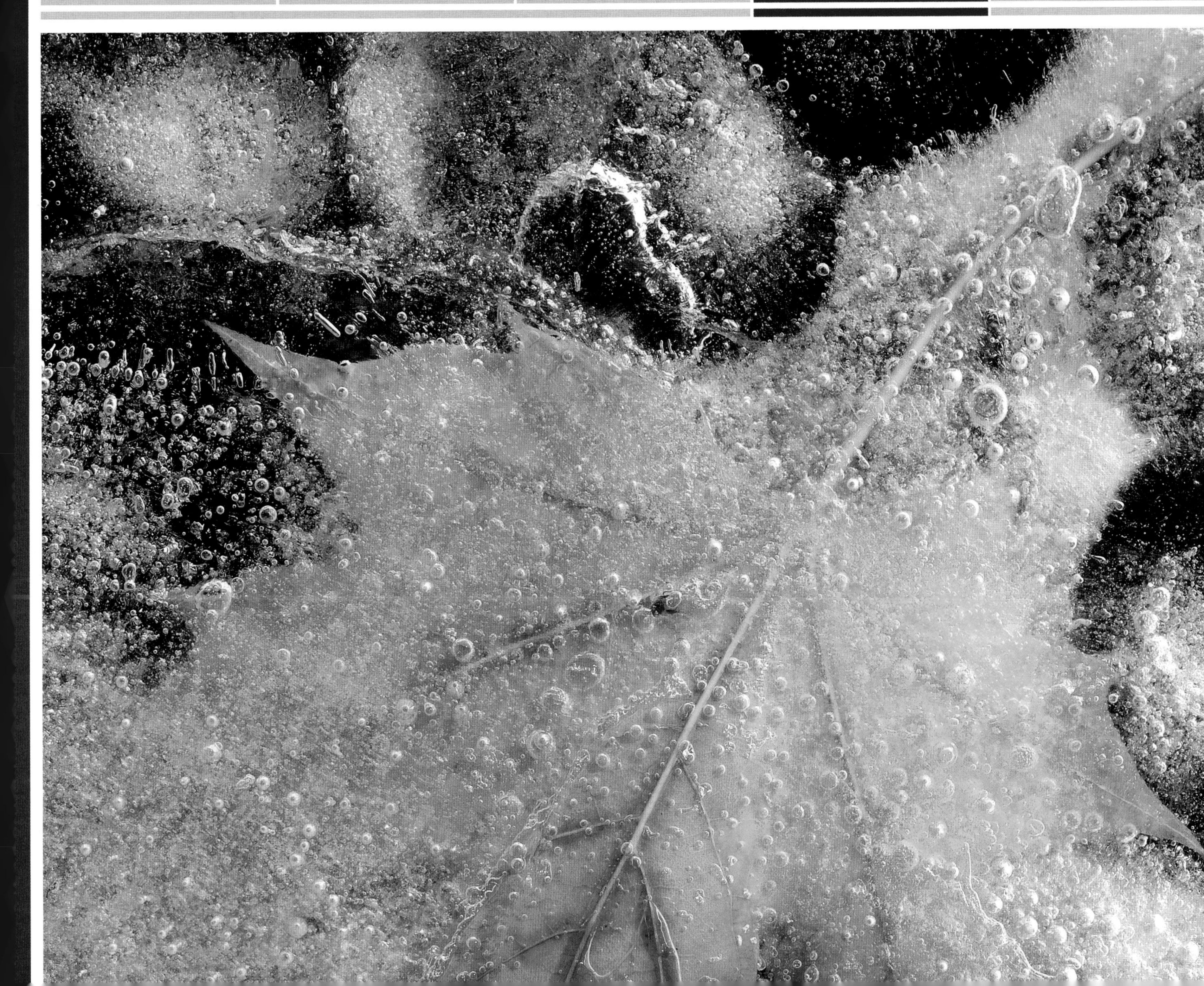

SETTING UP (ABOVE & RIGHT): Positioning your camera above the frozen leaf enables you to shoot it on the ground from a sturdy position, while taking full advantage of the natural light. The bright, reflective ice fooled my TTL metering system into underexposing the image, so I had to dial in a +1 stop exposure compensation to get my result.

Essential kit

MACRO LENS OR CLOSE-UP FILTER?

A lens that can focus relatively close is ideal for taking frame-filling shots of your frozen object. In this instance, I opted for a macro lens, but the tele-end of a standard zoom should prove fine if you are photographing a large subject, like a maple or sycamore leaf. However, if you still need to get closer, consider using an inexpensive close-up filter. A +3 dioptre should be fine, with versions from Hoya and Kood available for around £10-£15. To maximise image quality when using a close-up filter, select a mid-range aperture in the region of f/8-f/11.

Depth-of-field

When shooting static, flat subjects, your shutter speed is immaterial – as long as you have a sturdy support. Instead, aperture should be your priority. For this shot, you only need moderate depth-of-field, so f/11 is ideal

1 First, you'll need to find a suitable subject. Leaves are the most obvious subject to freeze, being something that you might find naturally frozen in a puddle, or the edge of a lake at this time of year. A maple leaf caught my eye, thanks to its colour and interesting shape. However, you may well have other ideas, and just about anything will work, from a feather to a pine cone.

2 Pour some water into your dish and place it in the freezer – ensuring it is lying flat so that it freezes evenly. Carefully place your subject centrally in the water – if it freezes too near the edge, it will restrict your composition. Once the water's frozen, add a little warm water and refreeze. This will help create cracks and air bubbles in the ice, adding interest to your final shot.

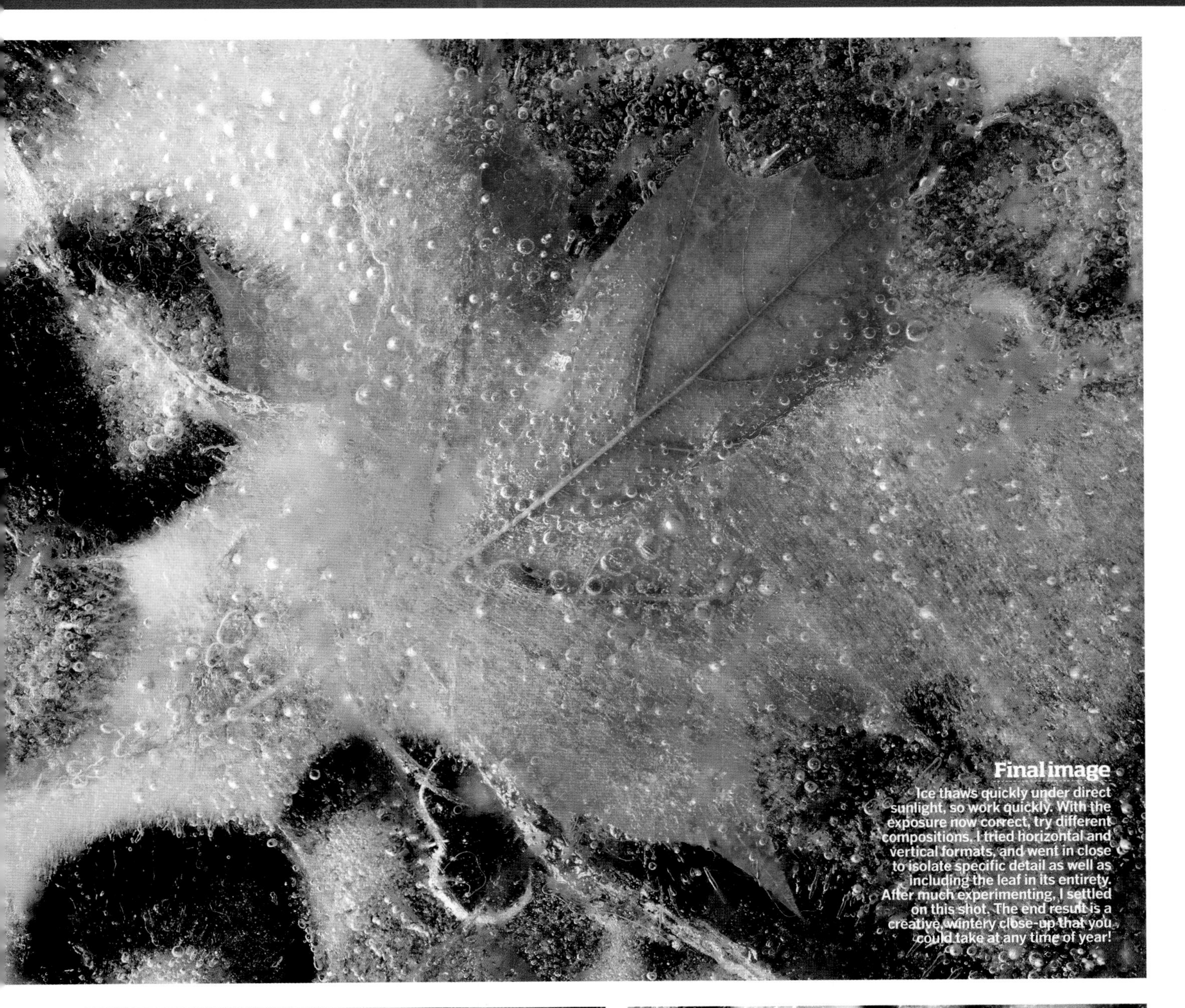

Final image

Ice thaws quickly under direct sunlight, so work quickly. With the exposure now correct, try different compositions. I tried horizontal and vertical formats, and went in close to isolate specific detail as well as including the leaf in its entirety. After much experimenting, I settled on this shot. The end result is a creative, wintery close-up that you could take at any time of year!

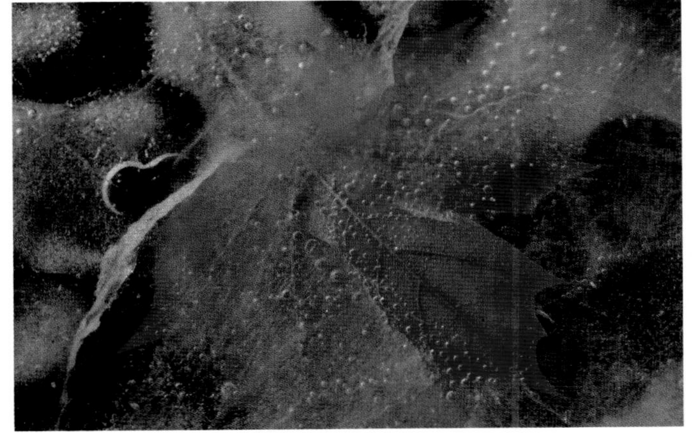

3 Once the water has frozen, you can begin snapping. You could shoot it indoors, using a lightbox to backlight it; but I opted to take it outside, so I could use the softness and warmth of the natural light. Using a tripod, I positioned my camera overhead, composed my shot and released the shutter. However, the brightly-lit ice fooled my metering system into underexposure.

4 To rectify the problem, I knew I needed to apply a degree of exposure compensation. As with most DSLRs, my camera has a dedicated exposure compensation facility. Using this, I selected a compensation of +1 stop. I took another photo and, having studied the result (and corresponding histogram) on my camera's LCD, I knew that the exposure was now correct.

Isn't it time you lost your head?

DANIEL LEZANO: There are numerous reasons for taking pictures, but sometimes you should do it just because it's fun. With this in mind, I decided to recreate an image I'd seen in a magazine that showed a headless body holding a head under one arm. It was quite a high-end image, so there was plenty of Photoshop involved to make it appear realistic, but I wanted to shoot a far more attainable image for anyone wanting to recreate a similar shot without having to spend ages in post-production. While this image does include a little Photoshop work, the emphasis is on careful composition and lighting to give the impression that there's only one person in the frame, and that they're holding their own head!

Get ready!

TIME REQUIRED
TEN MINUTES

EQUIPMENT USED
NIKON D700 WITH 50MM LENS, MANFROTTO 055MF4 TRIPOD WITH RC322 HEAD, BOWENS TWIN HEAD STUDIOFLASH

Studioflash lighting outfit

I could have used ambient light coming through the garage door and windows to light my subjects. But, I wanted to prevent as much light as possible from landing on the 'head' model's shoulders, so I needed more control over the light's direction. For this reason, I used two studioflash heads, one with a small softbox for a relatively wide, even spread of light, and the other with a small spill, which provided a narrow focus of light.

SETTING UP: There was no glamorous location for this portrait shoot, just the inside of a garage! The subjects, Hayley (the headless torso) and Katie (the head) were placed a metre or so from the white garage wall, with Hayley standing and Katie sat on top of a couple of sofa cushions. Both had been asked to wear black, as this would help with merging the two figures together to give the impression of a floating head. The windows of the garage had to be blocked off with parcel paper to minimise ambient light. For this image to work, I had to illuminate Hayley's neck and torso with one flashhead and Katie's head with the other. I fitted the softbox to the 500W studioflash and, with it at Hayley's head height, tilted it upwards slightly to reduce the amount of light reaching Katie's head. I fitted a spill to the 250W flash and placed this low and close to Katie, so that the light was concentrated on her head, with as little lighting as possible on her shoulders. A snoot or spotlight would have been a better option, but I lacked both. You can see the optimum position of the lights on the image on the right.

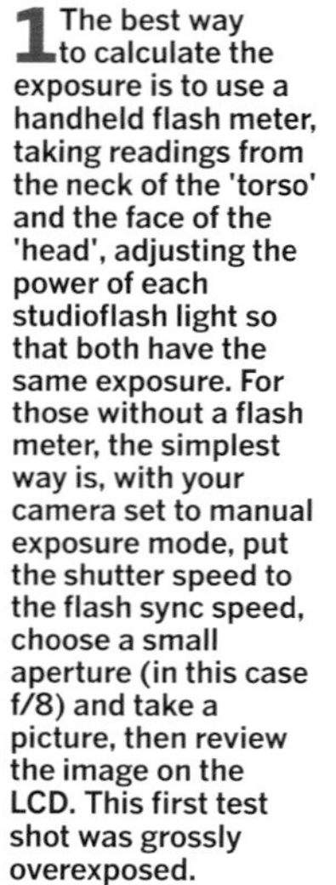

1 The best way to calculate the exposure is to use a handheld flash meter, taking readings from the neck of the 'torso' and the face of the 'head', adjusting the power of each studioflash light so that both have the same exposure. For those without a flash meter, the simplest way is, with your camera set to manual exposure mode, put the shutter speed to the flash sync speed, choose a small aperture (in this case f/8) and take a picture, then review the image on the LCD. This first test shot was grossly overexposed.

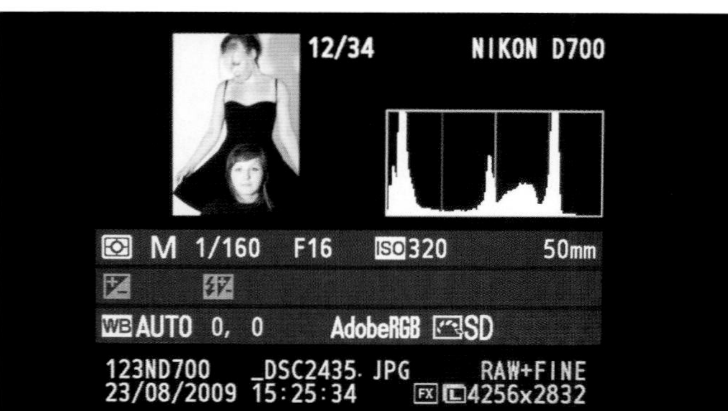

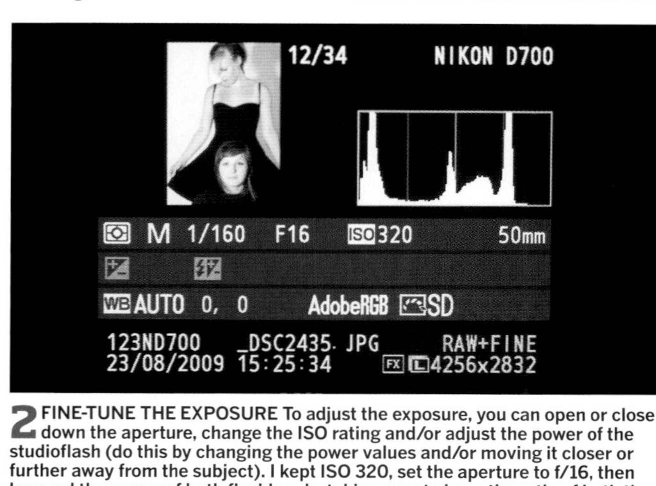

2 FINE-TUNE THE EXPOSURE To adjust the exposure, you can open or close down the aperture, change the ISO rating and/or adjust the power of the studioflash (do this by changing the power values and/or moving it closer or further away from the subject). I kept ISO 320, set the aperture to f/16, then lowered the power of both flashheads, taking care to keep the ratio of both the same. A couple more test shots and minor adjustments to the power gave a decent exposure, which I confirmed by checking the histogram.

3 With the lighting and exposure sorted, it was time to position the models so that the image was as realistic as possible. The key area I had to keep an eye on was getting the head's height correct so that the arms looked natural and not stretched out. It was also important to have the hands positioned so that they appear to be holding up the head, as well as also covering up as much of the neck area as possible. I asked Hayley to keep her chin up so that her neck is stretched out. Once I was happy with the set-up, I fired off a few different images, getting Hayley to adjust her hands to find the best position.

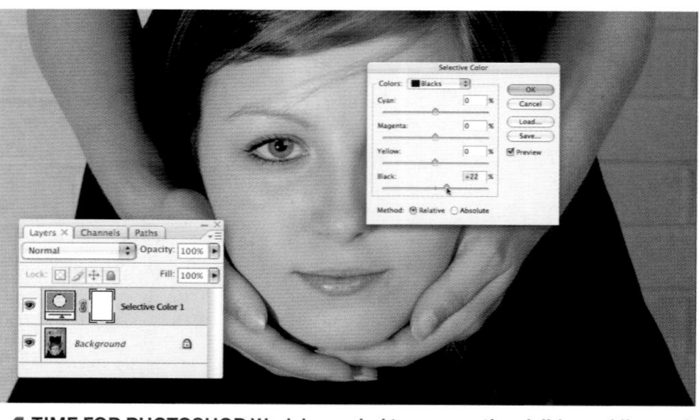

4 TIME FOR PHOTOSHOP Work is needed to remove the visible neckline and detail from the T-shirt. For the neckline, using the Polygonal Lasso Tool, I make a selection around the neckline area. Now I select the Paint Brush Tool and, while holding down the Alt key, click on an area of black, which selects that colour, and begin to paint out the skin. To merge the dress and T-shirt detail, I go to Layer>New Adjustment Layer>Selective Color, creating a new layer and preserving the original image. I select Blacks in the drop-down menu, then move the Black slider until all the detail has merged. Finally, using the Erase Tool, I delete any areas where wanted detail has been lost, such as the face and arms, restoring detail still preserved on the layer beneath.

Final image
And there we have it! An image that appears to show a headless torso holding a head. Why not try something similar with members of your family come Halloween!

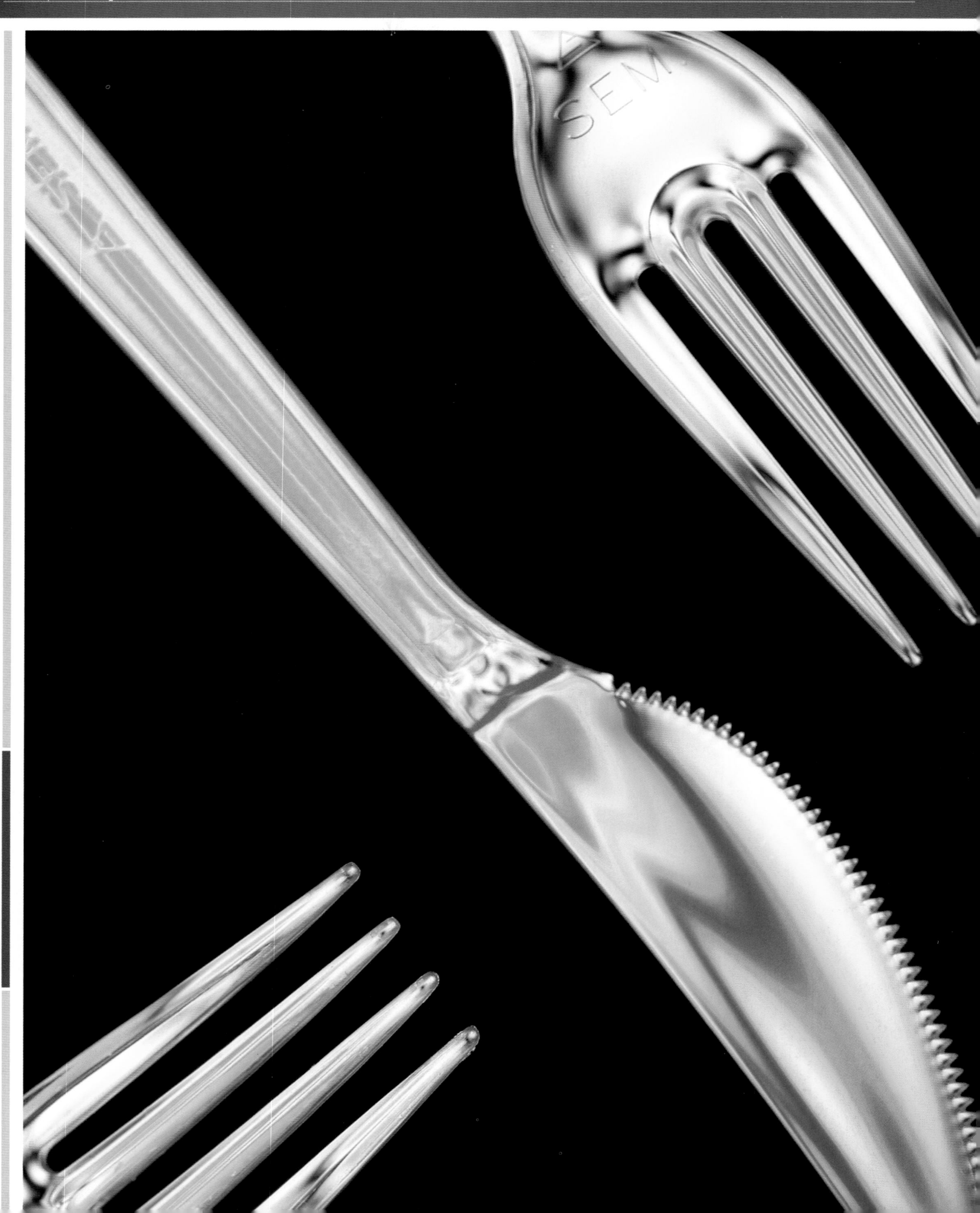

Make plastic fantastic!

DANIEL LEZANO: Cross-polarisation is a great technique to try at home as it's a relatively simple one to do. The idea is to 'sandwich' plastic objects between polarising material, to reveal stress patterns within the plastic as a kaleidoscopic feast of wonderful colours. It's a great way of creating extraordinary images of very ordinary subjects – in this case some clear plastic cutlery that I picked up at the local supermarket for £1! As you'll need to shoot in a darkened room, it's a technique you can try in the comfort of your own home at night.

Get ready!

TIME REQUIRED
15 MINUTES

EQUIPMENT NEEDED
CANON EOS 400D
100MM MACRO LENS
MANFROTTO TRIPOD
LIGHTBOX, POLARISING GEL & POLARISING FILTER

ALSO USED
PLASTIC CUTLERY
LENS CLEANING CLOTH

Essential kit

TRIPOD, LIGHTBOX & CLOTH!
I used a macro lens to get in really close to small areas of my subject, but the tele-end of a standard zoom would be suitable too. You'll need to use a tripod, as exposures will run into seconds, so a remote release is useful too, though I used the self-timer and mirror lock-up facility of my Canon EOS 400D to minimise shake. A lightbox provides all the light you'll need and, apart from the polarisers, you're almost there. One extra bit of kit I'd recommend is a lens cloth and/or blower brush. Smears and dust will be obvious at such magnification!
Use aperture-priority mode, start at f/8 for optimum sharpness, but feel free to change the aperture, to vary depth-of-field. Multi-zone metering will work here, but apply exposure compensation if needed.

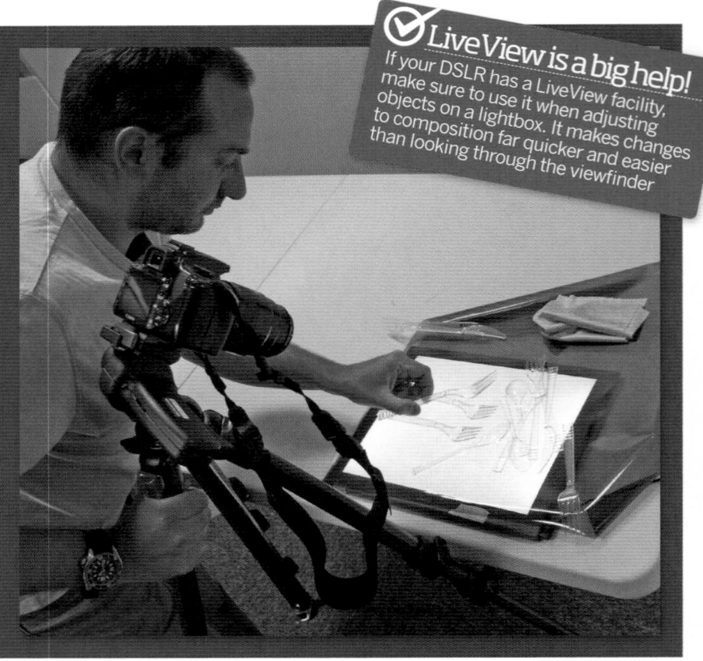

LiveView is a big help!

If your DSLR has a LiveView facility, make sure to use it when adjusting objects on a lightbox. It makes changes to composition far quicker and easier than looking through the viewfinder

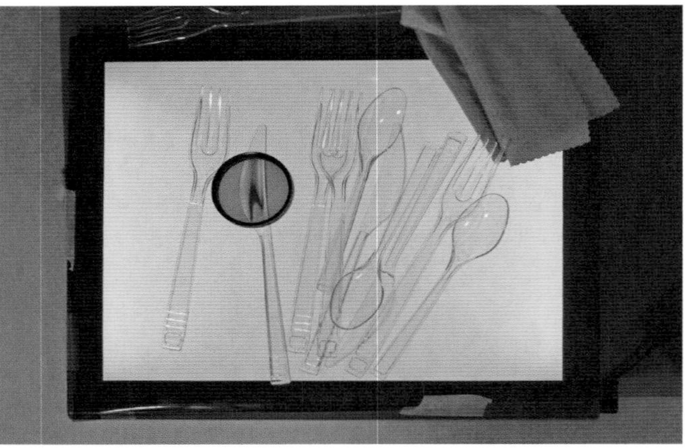

1 **Cross-polarisation is all about revealing stress fractures in plastic, so colours will play a very strong part in the success of the final image. However, equally important is the shape of the subject you choose, which will add extra interest to the composition. Choosing subjects with very defined outlines really works – for this step-by-step, I decided to shoot a cutlery set.**

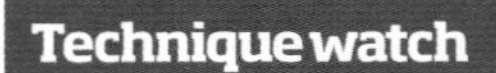

Technique watch

CROSS-POLARISATION
This technique involves placing a plastic subject between two polarisers. The easiest way to do this is to have a circular polarising filter attached to your lens and then have another polariser resting on a lightbox, with the plastic object(s) on top. You can use another screw-in polarising filter on the lightbox, but it limits the size of the subject you can use. A better alternative is to buy a sheet of polarising gel, which covers the whole lightbox surface. They're a little pricy in the UK, but we've been told by readers of an internet firm in the Far East (www.3dlens.com) that offers a good quality, affordable option.

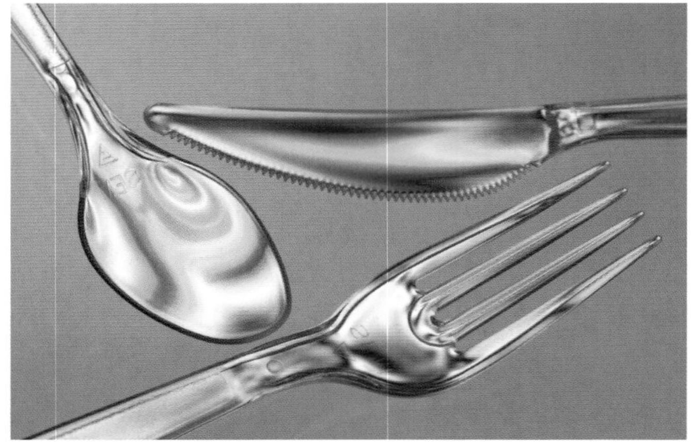

2 **It's worth jotting down a list of set-ups before you start and add to it as you go along – as you'll discover, once you start, you'll be changing the arrangement of objects, zooming in and out (or raising the tripod up and down) as you think up new angles to try. Start off with a simple composition like this and be more creative as you get the hang of things.**

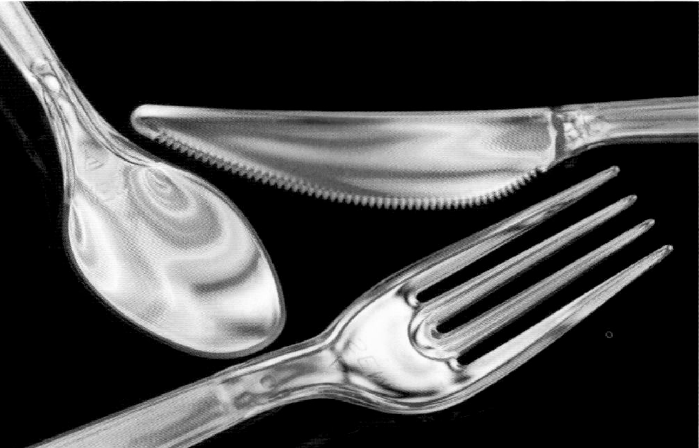

3 **Once you've set up the composition, look through the viewfinder (or better still use LiveView) and rotate the ring of the circular polarising filter. As if by magic, you'll see the background change from white to black and colours transform your plastic subjects. Stop turning the ring once you've a solid black background and the most intense colours and shoot away!**

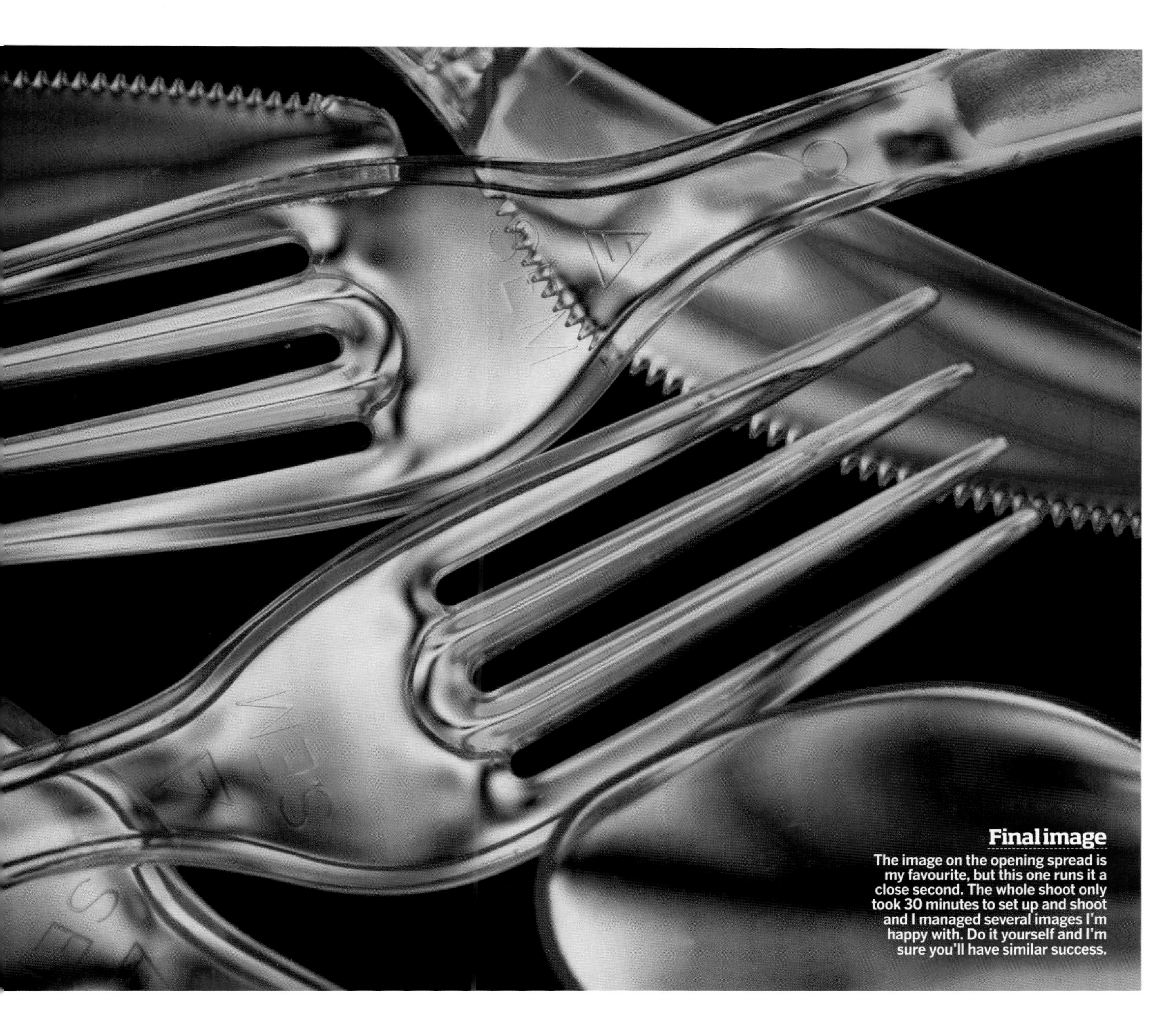

Final image

The image on the opening spread is my favourite, but this one runs it a close second. The whole shoot only took 30 minutes to set up and shoot and I managed several images I'm happy with. Do it yourself and I'm sure you'll have similar success.

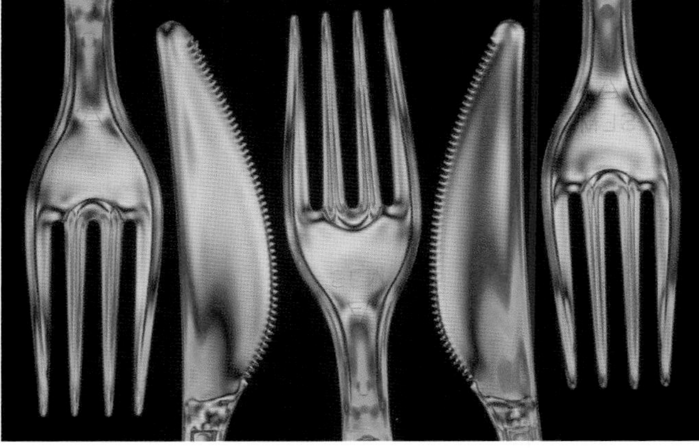

4 As I went through my list of shots, I started to concentrate more on the fork and the knife, as their distinct shapes made them far more photogenic than the spoon. As well as shooting from directly above the lightbox, I then tried lowering the tripod and shooting from an angle. I also tried using a wide aperture to reduce depth-of-field to vary my effects.

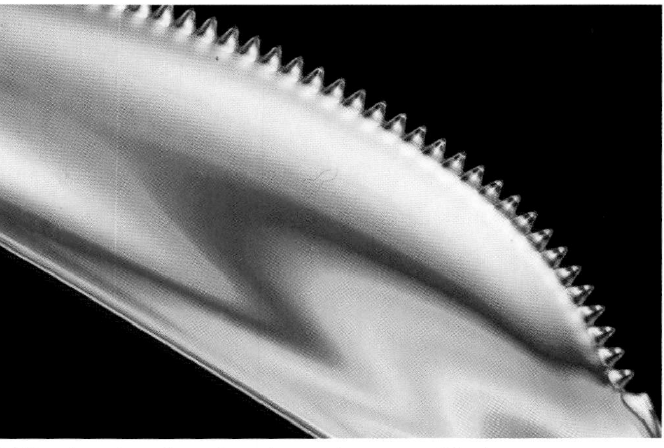

5 Despite trying to keep the cutlery as clean as possible, there was no way of preventing dust and fluff, floating through the air, from settling on it. It's worth doing a quick clean every couple of minutes as it's a far quicker option than having to remove dust and debris in Photoshop. The problem is accentuated when you start shooting macro close-ups such as this.

Blur your vision!

DANIEL LEZANO: Photoshop has allowed all sorts of weird and wonderful effects to be applied to images in post-production, but I still prefer to get as close as possible to the final image in-camera. Much of this is because I'm not particularly good with Photoshop to be honest, but mainly because I actually find it fun (as well as occasionally frustrating), to go 'old-school' and use more traditional photographic techniques to give the results I'm looking for. I've recently started experimenting with producing unusual soft-focus effects by smearing Vaseline on a filter. As I discovered, it's very easy to try, so why not give it a go and see how you get on.

Get ready!

TIME REQUIRED
30 MINUTES

EQUIPMENT NEEDED
CANON EOS 400D
SIGMA 70-200MM LENS
MANFROTTO TRIPOD
UV FILTER, LENS CLOTH

ALSO USED
POT OF VASELINE

1 The first thing you need to do is to find a suitable scene. Ideally, the location you choose should have some well-defined shapes and areas of strong shadows and bright highlights, such as woodland. However, this colourful field of poppies caught my eye and I hoped to be able to use the Vaseline to create a strong abstract effect based around the bold reds. I mounted my DSLR on a tripod, to ensure images were shake-free, and used Sigma's excellent 70-200mm f/2.8 lens to crop fairly tightly on the poppy field.

Essential kit

FILTER, VASELINE & CLOTH: This is a very affordable technique. A tub of Vaseline won't break the bank, but you'll need a UV or skylight filter to screw onto the front of your lens. I cannot over-emphasise how important it is that you apply Vaseline to the filter and not to the front element of your lens, as it could permanently damage the optics. You should also keep a clean lens cloth handy, for wiping away Vaseline when you want to clean the filter and try again, or at the end of your day's shooting. That's about all you need in terms of accessories, with the exception of a tripod, which will keep your camera steady when you're preparing the composition and focusing on the scene.

Technique watch

APPLYING VASELINE: As you'll discover, getting a desired effect requires lots of trial and error when it comes to smearing the filter. Start off by applying a thin line of Vaseline across the central part of the filter, and apply further smears until you've covered the whole surface. Take a few shots, rotate the filter so the smears are diagonal and shoot again. Apply thicker smears of Vaseline to create random patterns, and then wipe the filter clean and try again!

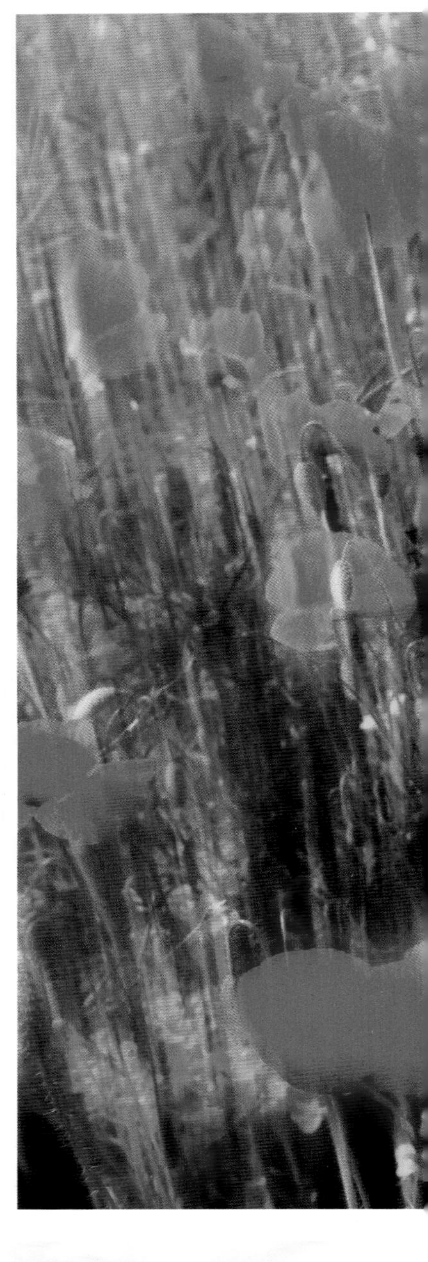

2 With the camera supported on a sturdy tripod, it's important to 'lock' the focus before smearing the filter with Vaseline – the AF system will struggle to focus once it's been applied. To do this, focus on the scene normally and then switch the lens from AF to manual focus, so when you press the shutter button later on, to take a shot, it won't affect the focusing.

3 With everything prepared, it's time to apply the Vaseline. Rather than scoop big wedges from the tub, gently smear relatively thin lines of Vaseline across the frame. Here, you can see how just a single smear affects the scene. I looked through the viewfinder the whole time I was applying the Vaseline, to see how it was affecting the overall scene.

Final image

My favourite image was one taken towards the end of my session. After refining my composition, angling the camera down towards a smaller area of the field (to make the poppies larger in the frame), I carefully applied very thin smears to the filter.

4 Once I'd applied the Vaseline across the filter, I fired off a few frames, choosing a variety of apertures from f/5.6 to f/13, so that I could see how the results varied (in truth, it made little difference). After a few frames, I used my finger to apply more Vaseline, to see if a thicker layer would improve the effect. However, I found that using too much of it led to too soft a result.

5 As well as horizontal smears, I also rotated the filter so as to make the smears run diagonally and then vertically – this made a big difference to the result. I also tried a variety of smear patterns, such as criss-crossed lines and wavy lines to see what effect it had on the scene. It's worth trying this, as it's impossible to predict what works best.

Outdoor Indoor Lighting Creative Photoshop

Create an illusion of scale

STEWART BYWATER: One technique that is quick, easy and really good fun, is to try and shoot a scale model so that, at first glance, it might trick the viewer into thinking that it is the real thing. It doesn't really matter what you choose as your miniature object, as long as you set it and shoot it in such a way that it looks in scale with its surroundings. I decided to shoot a model car, as I already have a few at home. They are also ideal for a quick shoot, as you don't need to build any sets or scout around for a good location – you can literally take them out to the street outside your house and shoot them from the pavement. Just about any model car could be used, but if you want the result to look more realistic, it obviously makes sense to find a model that is well-detailed and correctly proportioned. This often means choosing a larger model, rather than something matchbox-sized. This also helps when it comes to making it look large in the frame.

There are several factors to watch out for, as it is easy to overlook a small detail in the frame that may betray the true size of your car, such as large-grained pavements (it will be obvious that the car is very close to the surface, and therefore a miniature); traffic bollards and lamp posts, and other vehicles (whether passing or stationary). Another thing to be aware of is capturing your own reflection or shadow in the shot. As you will be shooting from very close to the model, it's actually quite difficult to keep these out of the shot. If you are using a wide-angle lens (recommended), you want to shoot at its minimum focusing distance.

Although not essential, I'd recommend taking a friend along for this sort of shot, as when shooting from ground level, it is difficult to watch out for oncoming vehicles and pedestrians. They could also keep an eye on your kit bag, to make sure nobody makes off with it!

Finally, it is worth wearing scruffy clothes for this sort of shot, as you will inevitably end up getting dirty when you're lying on the ground.

Essential kit

HOODMAN RIGHT-ANGLE VIEWER:
If you're shooting with your camera at ground-level (or at any angle from which looking through the viewfinder is difficult), a right-angle viewer can make a huge difference. Not only does it make composing certain shots much easier (and therefore more enjoyable), but it also relieves strain on the neck, whilst allowing you to keep your head in a more natural position (and off the ground). I used the Hoodman right-angle viewer, which is available from Newpro UK for around £99. For further information, or to see other products from Hoodman, visit the Newpro UK website at: www.newprouk.co.uk.

TIME REQUIRED
20 MINUTES

EQUIPMENT
CANON EOS 5D WITH CANON 17-40MM ZOOM HOODMAN ANGLE VIEWER

ALSO USED
TOY CAR

Technique watch

DEPTH-OF-FIELD: The area in focus is key to making this picture look believable; too much or too little will betray the real size of the model and diminish the effect. As you will be shooting at a very short distance from the subject, the depth-of-field will be minimal anyway. If it is too shallow and too much of the car falls out of focus, the result will automatically look like a macro shot. Inversely, this shallow focus technique can be used to make real-life scenes look like models. If you use too small an aperture, the depth-of-field will extend back too far and leave the surroundings in sharp focus, exposing the fact that this is only a very small area you are photographing. Due to these tiny margins it is important to bracket your shots at various apertures, as you may not be able to see exactly where the focus falls off on the LCD screen.

1 Having chosen your miniature subject, the first thing you'll need to do is find a suitable location. If the buildings are too big or too close, they will dwarf your subject, but too small or far away, and they will be virtually unidentifiable in the shot, and therefore not worth including at all. Once you have placed your subject, it's time to assume the shooting position.

2 Set your camera to aperture-priority mode and start with an aperture of around f/5.6. This should be enough to keep most of the car in focus, while blurring the immediate background, from the tarmac to the buildings behind. Keeping the aperture fairly wide will blur the area in front of the car too, which will help to hide any textures that may diminish the effect.

Wear old clothes!

If you know that you're going to be shooting a subject that will require you to kneel or lie on the ground, it is worth wearing some scruffy old clothes or taking a rug or dustbin liner with you

Final image

Using a wide-angle zoom allows me to fill a large portion of the frame with my subject, while including some of the large houses in the background to add a sense of scale. While it's obvious after close inspection that it's a model car, at first glance it is not so apparent. When shooting, it is vital to get down to pavement level. This 'real-life' viewpoint makes the car seem larger than it is, as when I shot from only slightly above the car, it instantly appeared smaller.

3 My first attempt, using a 90mm macro lens, didn't quite work. I took it with the camera almost resting on the surface of the pavement. The macro lens made the car look quite realistic, but the depth-of-field was so shallow (because I had to shoot so close to the car) that the buildings in the background were unidentifiable, so the image had no real sense of scale.

4 An ultra wide-angle zoom (in this case a Canon 17-40mm f/4L) gives more believable results. Once again, I got down as low as I could, with the camera virtually resting on the pavement, and shot from as close to the car as the lens focus would allow. I zoomed in slightly to make the car fill a good portion of the frame, whilst including a fair amount of background detail to add scale.

No strings attached!

MATTY GRAHAM: I recently stumbled across a film I had watched at the movies when I was a child: Memoirs Of An Invisible Man. It always made me chuckle when the star, Chevy Chase, unwrapped his bandages and all the viewer could see was a hat, specs and coat 'floating' in mid air. The movie got me thinking of how to recreate a similar effect in a photo. Without Hollywood special effects, I chose to use thin fishing line and a boom stand to suspend my breakfast crockery as if an invisible waiter was serving it up. The trick with this technique is to use as few wires as possible and a solid background as, when you come to removing the wires in Photoshop, the plainer the backdrop, the easier it is to clone accurately. You don't have to copy my idea as the creative possibilities around your own home are endless!

Get ready!

TIME REQUIRED
45 MINUTES

EQUIPMENT NEEDED
CANON EOS 5D WITH 50MM F/1.8 LENS

ALSO USED
FISHING LINE, STICKY TAPE, BOOM STAND, PROPS & TRIPOD

SETTING UP: I chose to position my set-up in the garden. This is a great location, but remember that objects that are suspended by the fishing lines may swing in the wind, so try and shelter your props to keep them still.

1 I started by placing my boom stand (you could also use a tripod) into position. Because I was shooting on a very sunny day, I had to place it to the right of the frame so that its shadow was not visible in the image.

Essential tool

CLONING TOOL:
The Cloning Tool is one of the most effective weapons in the Photoshop armory. Users can select how hard they want the cloning brush to be and also its opacity. You can even clone from separate images so, for example, if you have a portrait where one of your model's eyes is closed, you can graft them in from an additional image.

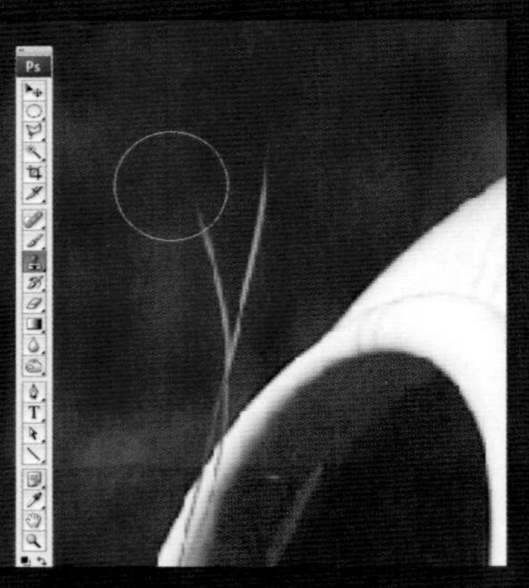

2 Next up, I cut some fishing line from the spool and wrapped it around the teapot. I then raised the teapot into its 'floating' position above the table and tied the other end to the boom stand using a secure knot.

3 The teapot was in the right position, but there was a problem! The fishing wire couldn't support the weight of the teapot and snapped. The solution was to cut a new strip and 'double up' the wire to make it much stronger.

4 Next, I added a cup and spoon to fit in with the breakfast theme. I found the mug kept falling forward, so used sticky tape to fix the fishing line to the back of the mug so it balanced in a more natural, upright position.

Final image

There we have it, breakfast served up by an invisible waiter. Chevy would be proud!

5 I took a test shot and reviewed it on my LCD screen. The shot was good, but the background was cluttered. The solution was to raise the tripod up to get rid of the brown fence and just include the grass as the background.

6 With the shot captured, I opened the image in Photoshop ready to clone out the fishing lines. I then made a duplicate layer (Ctrl&J) to work on just in case I made a mistake and needed to start over using the original layer.

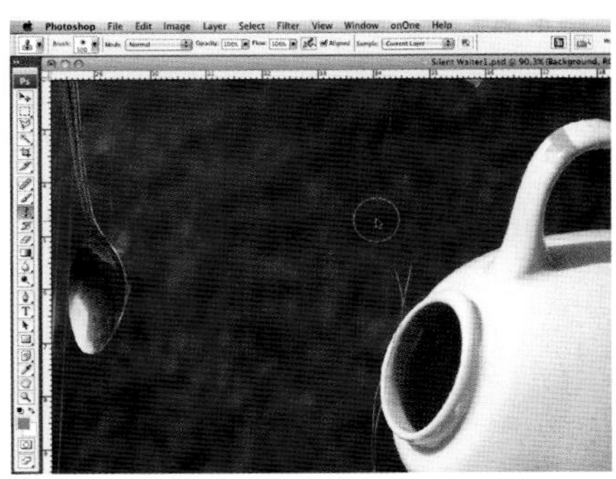

7 I selected the Cloning Tool and, after zooming in closer to the image, began to clone out the lines that were holding up my props. It's important to take your time with this step and clone carefully. I then flattened and saved my file.

Make your own lighting masks

DANIEL LEZANO: Whoever coined the phrase 'the camera never lies' really didn't have a clue. The fact is, deception has long been a staple diet of the photographer, with all sorts of tricks being employed to fool viewers into believing that an image is something it isn't. Nowadays, we would automatically think of the various post-processing alterations that are possible, but the truth is that there have always been lots of ways of faking a scene at the shooting stage. For instance, fitting a filter to your lens effectively takes the scene one step further away from reality, as does selecting a very slow shutter speed to blur moving water into a milky mist.

In this photo project, we'll be looking at how making your own cardboard mask to place in front of a studioflash head can allow you to create a lighting effect that gives the illusion of a venetian window blind. It's a very simple technique to try and the results can look effective when done properly, adding an air of mood and mystery to your portraits.

Get ready!

TIME REQUIRED
ONE HOUR

EQUIPMENT
CANON EOS 550D WITH CANON EF 17-40MM F/4L USM LENS

ALSO USED
CARDBOARD MASK, SCALPEL, ELINCHROM D-LITE IT KIT & LIGHTING STAND

'Here's one I made earlier...': Creating your lighting mask

The easiest way to make a mask is to cut it out from the side of a cardboard box. You'll need it to be as large as possible to ensure the light reaching the subject passes through the openings you cut, rather than around the side of the mask. To make this venetian blind mask, I drew straight lines at regular intervals, then cut them using a scalpel and cutting mat (you can also use scissors) to give a rectangular mask with several similarly sized apertures.
It's important to ensure the edges of the apertures are cut as smooth and straight as possible as any major imperfections may show up on the shadows cast. Once you've made your mask, fix it to a lighting pole using sellotape. Try to tape it to one section of the stand, as this makes it easier to raise and lower the stand, which you'll need to do to position the areas of light and shadow on the subject.

Technique watch

HARD AND SOFT SHADOWS: You can vary how hard or how soft the shadows fall on the scene by your choice of lighting attachment and the position of the mask. Using a softbox will give a softer, more indistinct effect, while using a spill will give a more focused and direct light that produces a harder shadow. You'll find you can also increase the hardness of the shadows by moving the mask towards the subject, or soften shadows by moving it towards the light. The choice is yours.

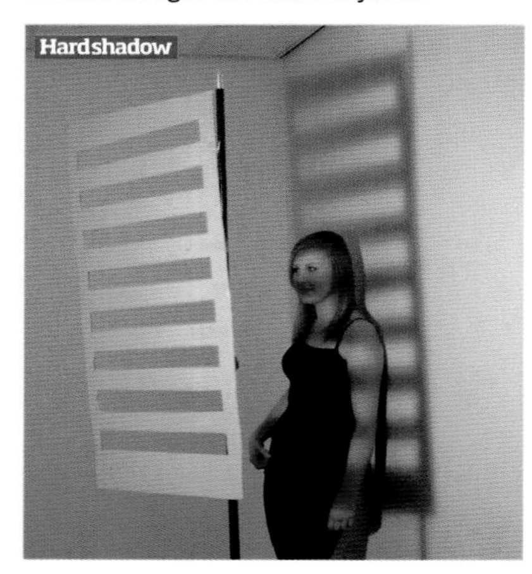
Hard shadow

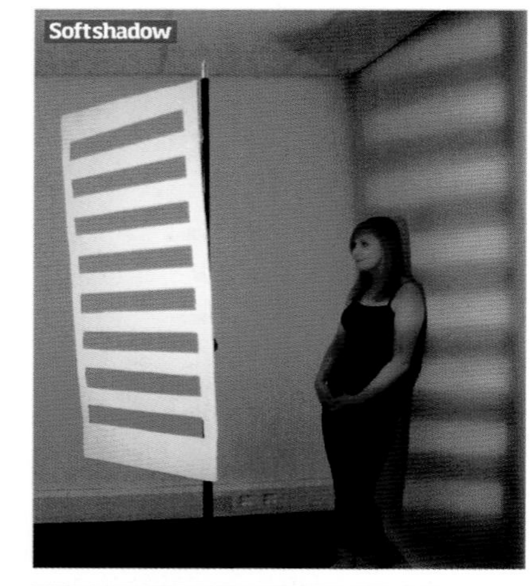
Soft shadow

Final image

The third position of the mask gave a far more pleasing result and I also preferred the composition with the camera used in landscape format rather than held upright.

1 Work out exposure using a flash meter (or by trial and error by changing the aperture setting with the camera in manual and the shutter speed set to the flash sync). My set-up gave a exposure of 1/160sec at f/16 (ISO 100).

2 Place your mask between the studioflash head and the area where you will position your subject. Take a shot and review the result. In this shot the shadows were hardly visible, so the mask was moved closer to the subject.

3 The next shot gave far more defined lines of shadows but now the result was too harsh, so the mask was moved away from the subject. Take care when moving the mask, as if the angle changes, the shadow lines may become uneven.

Coat your own!

LEE FROST: Back in the days when photographers did it by hand in the dark (printing that is!), I enjoyed coating heavy art paper with a liquid photographic emulsion before printing black & white images onto it. It was a fiddly and messy process (aren't most things done in the dark?) but the results had a wonderful fine-art quality that made the effort worthwhile. Fortunately, you no longer need a darkroom to experiment with hand-coating, because inkjet pre-coats are now available that allow you to make a wide range of materials receptive to inkjet inks, allowing you to go ahead and print photographs on them. Paper is an obvious choice of material, but if you feel more ambitious, and your printer has a flat-feed, you can print images on fabrics, wood, metal and glass. To get you started, we'll concentrate on using pre-coats on paper, to show you not only how easy this technique is, but also how effective it can be.

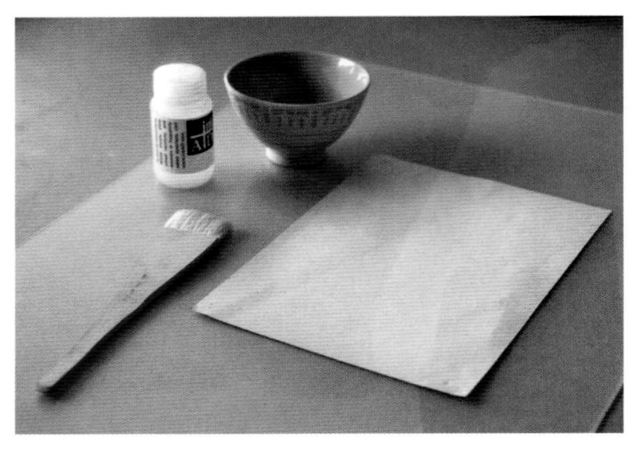

SETTING UP: Find yourself a clear area to work in, away from anything expensive, with plenty of light, so you can see what you're doing. Put down a wipe-clean mat or some newspaper to work on. You'll need a bowl to put your coating solution in, and a clean, wide brush to apply it to your paper surface.

Get ready!

TIME REQUIRED
1 HOUR

EQUIPMENT
INKAID INKJET PRECOATS
EPSON STYLUS PRO 4800
PRINTER BRUSH & PAPER

Essential kit

INKJET PRE-COATS: Although there's nothing to stop you from printing photographs on ordinary paper or card, the images usually end up looking flat and blurry because the ink soaks into the substrate and spreads out, a bit like ink on blotting paper. Similarly, if you print on a non-porous material such as plastic or metal, ink will stay on the surface of the substrate and probably be smeared by the printer. To prevent this, special pre-coats have been developed that make both porous and non-porous materials receptive to inkjet inks and allow you to print high quality images on them without falling foul of any of these problems. It's a simple concept, but it works brilliantly, and has opened up all sorts of creative avenues for photographers. Ottawa Speciality Coatings Corporation was the first to launch inkjet pre-coats, under the inkAID label (www.inkaid1.com). You can buy a sample pack of inkAID pre-coats for £25.95 plus postage, from Artvango (www.artvango.co.uk). The kit contains six 118ml bottles of: Clear Semi-Gloss, Clear Gloss, White Matte, Iridescent Gold, Clear Gloss Type II (with adhesive) and a separate adhesive pre-coat for use with the Clear Gloss pre-coat. Each bottle contains enough pre-coat to prepare a dozen or more sheets of A4 paper, with two coats on each sheet, so there's more than enough to get you going. I found the White Matte and Clear Semi-Gloss pre-coats to be the most useful for photographic printing, so you could bypass the sample pack and order individual bottles.

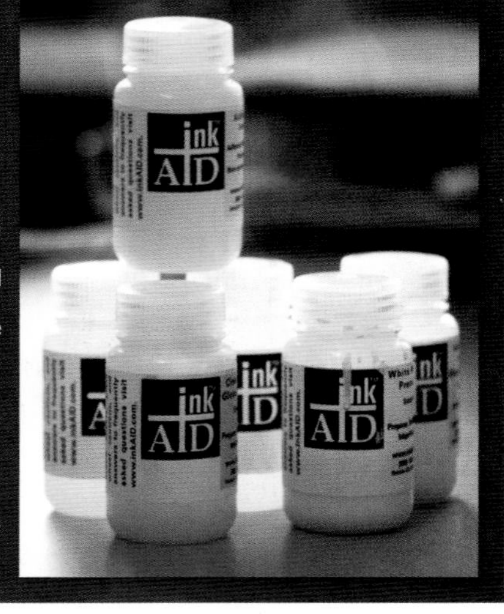

1 The first step is to choose your paper. This is where you can experiment. Try textured art paper, watercolour paper, handmade paper, coloured paper, etc. The yellowing endpapers from old books also work well if you want to create prints with a distinct vintage look – as long as it will feed through your printer, it's worth trying.

2 Now it's time to apply the pre-coats. A clear, wipe-clean work area is required, though any spills and splashes are easy to wipe up. The bottle of pre-coat should also be given a good shake before pouring a small quantity into a clean plastic dish. This can all be done in daylight, as the pre-coats aren't light-sensitive.

3 To apply the pre-coat, you just paint it on, trying to avoid getting hairs or other debris trapped in the emulsion, and also making sure that the pre-coating is applied evenly. That said, if you intentionally want to see brush strokes and texture in the pre-coat, you can apply a thicker layer and be more random with your strokes.

Mixed media

If you're feeling really ambitious, you could use coatings to create mixed-media artworks by printing on pages of text, handwritten letters or manuscripts, maps, illustrations or paintings!

4 Once thoroughly dry, apply a second coat, ideally brushing at 90° to the direction of the first coat if you want an even finish. Once two coats have been applied, and each sheet is fully dried, place them between the pages of a big book, weighed down with more books, or any other flat, heavy object, and leave everything overnight.

5 By the next morning, the sheets will be flat and ready for use. To print on the coated paper, treat it like normal inkjet paper. The printer settings required will depend on the printer you use, the material you're printing on and your selection of pre-coat, but I find that Archival Matt or Watercolour Paper media settings work fine.

6 Allow the inks to dry overnight; then, as a final step, it is worth considering protecting the delicate print surfaces by applying two or three coats of print protection spray. I use Hahnemuehle Protective Spray, but other sprays, such as the Frogjuice Aerosol from Fotospeed and Permajet Inkjet Fixative will do the same job.

New Year Calendar

CAROLINE WILKINSON: As the end of each year approaches, we all face the tricky task of choosing a calendar that reflects our taste. Pretty pictures by photographers pack the shelves in this seasonal format, but why fork out cash for someone else's images when your photographs could do just as good a job!

Get ready!

TIME REQUIRED
30 MINUTES

EQUIPMENT NEEDED
IMAGES & PHOTOSHOP

ALSO USED
5X7IN 200GSM MATT PHOTO PAPER

Although it's a great way to showcase your images, your calendar will look better if you group your shots into themes such as family, flowers, wildlife or landscapes. There's no rule to say you should stick to the conventional 12-month calendar either: if you've got too many images to pick from, why not do a weekly or, if not enough images, a bi-monthly calendar. This step-by-step guide will show you how to design a desk-size version from scratch, but the basic principle applies for any size of calendar – simply substitute the 5x7in dimensions for an A4, or even A3, format in step one. If it's A4 you're after, we've helpfully provided an A4 calendar template for you on our website. You'll find it at www.digitalslrphoto.com.

Essential advice

FINISHING TOUCH: You could either get your calendar printed at a professional printers or do it at home on high-quality photographic paper (200gsm or more). There is no need to get a desk calendar ring-bound like you would with bigger calendars (though this can be easily done at most print stores), a picture stand will do the job. You can buy small picture stands/easels from most art stores, and there is a great assortment online to suit all tastes from vintage antique to simple wooden easels. But for a really cost-effective alternative, turn a plastic CD case inside out (so it stands upright) and slot the sheets of paper behind its grooves; however, this limits you to a vertical format calendar.

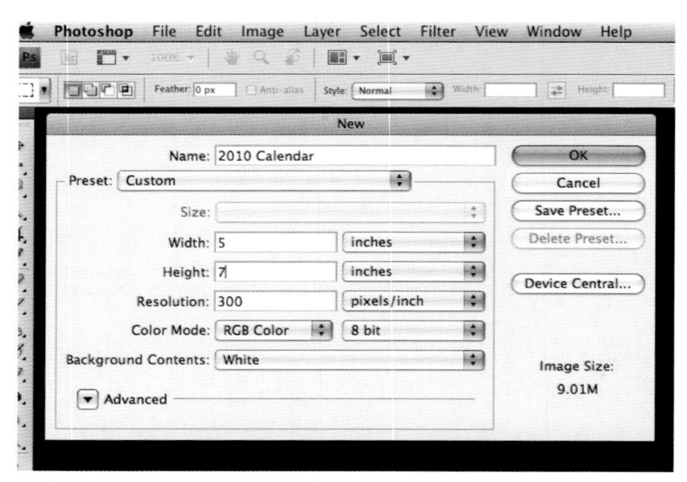

1 Having selected your collection of images, the first step is to create a template, which you can adapt for each month of your calendar. Create a new file (*File>New*) and select the size of the paper you want to print on. In this case, I'm using 5x7in photo paper and therefore set these dimensions under Width and Height, making sure Resolution is set at 300. Click OK.

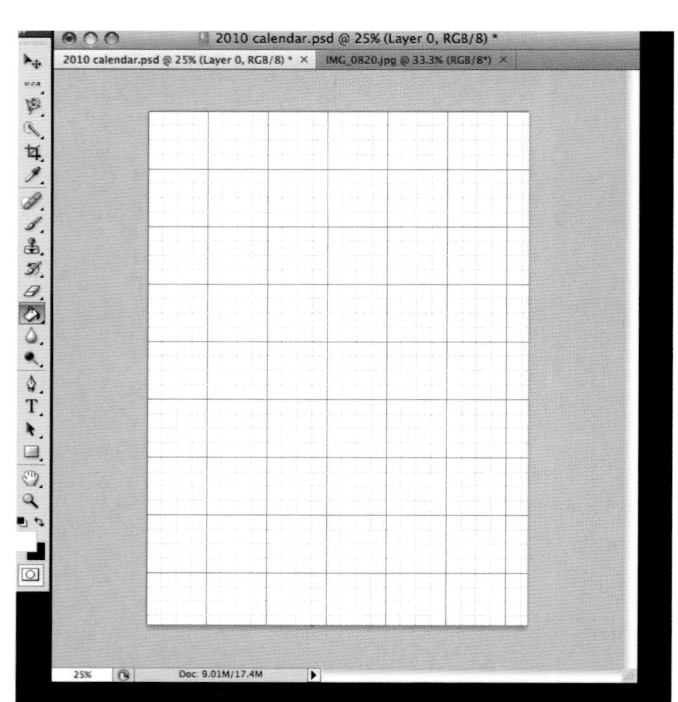

2 Decide whether you want a vertical or horizontal format; if horizontal go to *Image>Image Rotation>90 CW*. Using the Paint Bucket Tool, fill your Background Layer with the colour you want, unless you want to leave it white. I found it easier to judge where to place my image and diary dates on the page once I turned the Grid lines on (*View>Show>Grid*).

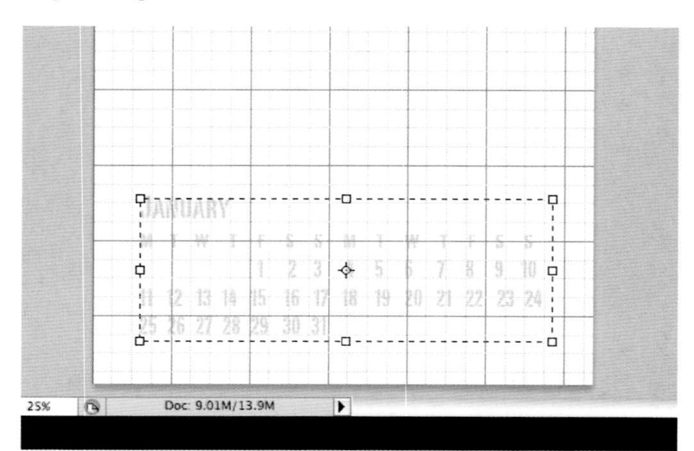

3 Next, create a text box with the Horizontal Type Tool. Use the grid lines as a guide: try to leave an equal amount of space on two sides of the text box for framing. Note: It looks better to have at least one grid box space between the edge of the page and the text. Select the font type, size and colour of your text and type in the month, days and dates you want.

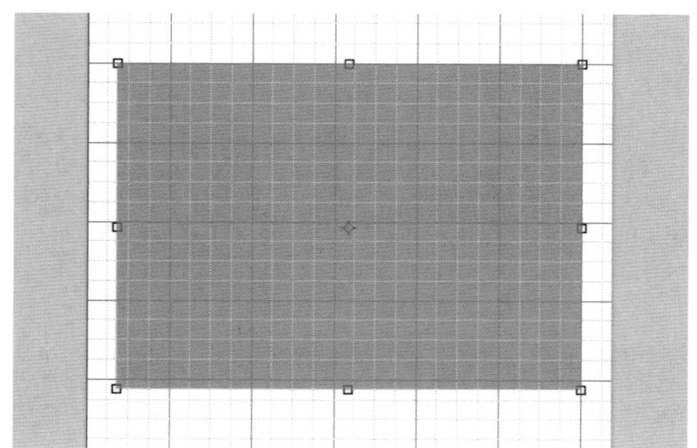

4 Now create a new layer (*Layer>New*), fill it with a contrasting colour to your Background Layer and use the Move Tool to resize it. For the best results, position the box in the opposite third of the page to the text box. This will be the template for your image box, which you can later adjust to fit the shape of your photo. Save the document as template.psd.

Digital SLR Photography

2012 CALENDAR

Now you're finished. Keep the template file for next year or use it to create a series of themed calendars as gifts to family and friends. For a professional touch, you could add a cover to your calendar by repeating the steps and adding a title, but leave out the dates. Also, why not try choosing a background colour that complements each image.

5 Open your first image in Photoshop and drag it – using the Move Tool – on to your calendar document. Then resize the image to fit into the image box, holding down Shift, to keep the image proportionate. If it's a portrait-format image use the top and bottom of the (grey) box as the boundary. Use your judgement here and the grid boxes to frame your photo.

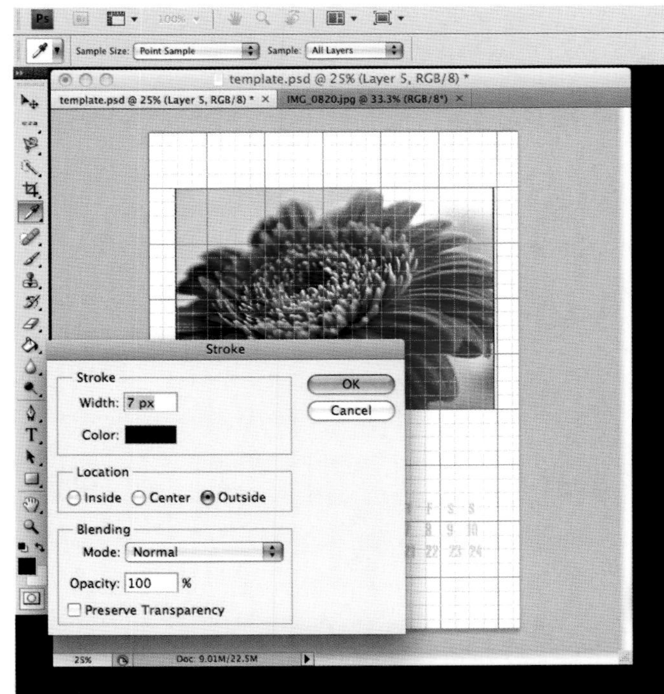

6 Click on your photo layer and go to *Edit>Stroke* and change width, colour and select Outside to create a border. Once you're happy with the first month's page, flatten the image (*Layer> Flatten Image*) and resave the file e.g January. TIFF. Now, re-open the template file and repeat steps 5 and 6 for each month, remembering to change the month and dates in the calendar.

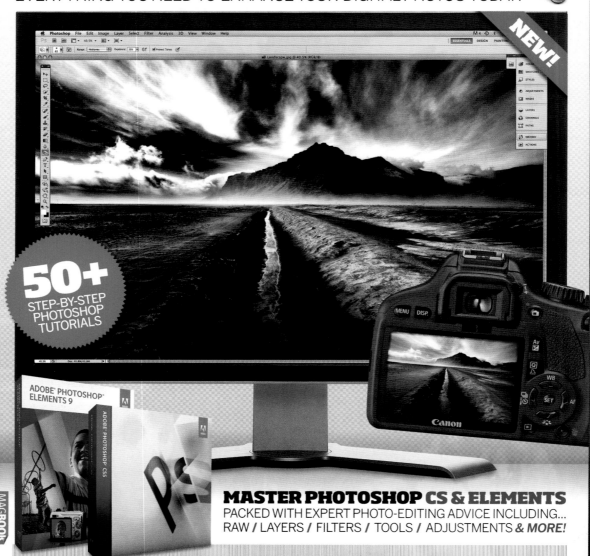

Step-by-step tutorials

PHOTOSHOP PROJECTS

OUR EASY TO FOLLOW PHOTOSHOP STEP-BY-STEPS WILL HELP YOU TRANSFORM YOUR IMAGES

Outdoor
Indoor
Lighting
Creative
Photoshop

Cross-processing in Photoshop

DANIEL LEZANO: Photoshop has allowed us to create all sorts of wonderful effects, but many photographers who grew up in the film age still hanker for some of the old favourites. The portrait enthusiasts among you may remember cross-processing, which involved developing a film in the 'wrong' chemistry, (i.e. running a slide film through chemicals meant for negatives, or developing print films in slide film chemistry). This would lead to some adventurous and very unusual results, such as particularly punchy colours or pale and tinted skin tones in your image. This technique was popular with fashion and 'lifestyle' photographers in the '90s and many digital photographers now successfully mimic the effect. Cross-processing film was always unpredictable and results varied according to film brands and film type – slide films gave very different results to cross-processed print films.

Outlined here is a simple, yet effective, technique for recreating the cross-processed look digitally in Photoshop. It makes use of the Curves adjustment, which means you'll need the full version of Photoshop, or a Curves plug-in for Adobe Elements.

Get ready!

TIME REQUIRED
15 MINUTES

EQUIPMENT NEEDED
NIKON D700
105MM F/2.8 LENS

ALSO USED
PHOTOSHOP CS3

Original

1 **Choose a portrait image you like, but one you feel would benefit from more visual impact. Select *Window>Layers* to reveal the Layers palette. Select the half white/half black icon that allows you to create a new Adjustment Layer and choose Curves from the drop-down menu. Note a new layer called Curves 1 appears above the Background Layer (original image).**

2 **A Curves box appears, which displays a histogram of the image, with a straight diagonal line running from bottom left (pure black) to top right (pure highlight). Above the histogram is an option tab called Channel that will currently read RGB. You'll use the Channel tab to select the individual channels in the following order: Red, Blue, then Green.**

3 **Select Red and drag the top right of the curve a little to the left. Then click two points around a third of the way from the top and bottom and drag them to create a gentle S curve (i.e. drag the top point slightly to the left and the bottom point to the right). This gives deeper shadows and brighter highlights in the Red channel – check the Preview button to see the effect.**

4 **Once you've adjusted the Red channel, click on the Channel drop-down menu and select the Blue channel. Pull the top right end of the curve downwards to remove some blue from the highlights. When you've done this, pull up the bottom of the curve by no more than half a square, to make the shadows in the blue channel a bit more solid. The line should remain straight.**

Colour experiments
Cross-processing films often gave very unpredictable results, so when you're working on the colour channels, don't be afraid to experiment with your channel tweaks to see what effects occur

Final image
Compare this picture to the original and the effect speaks for itself: an image that holds far more visual impact thanks to the extra colour and contrast.

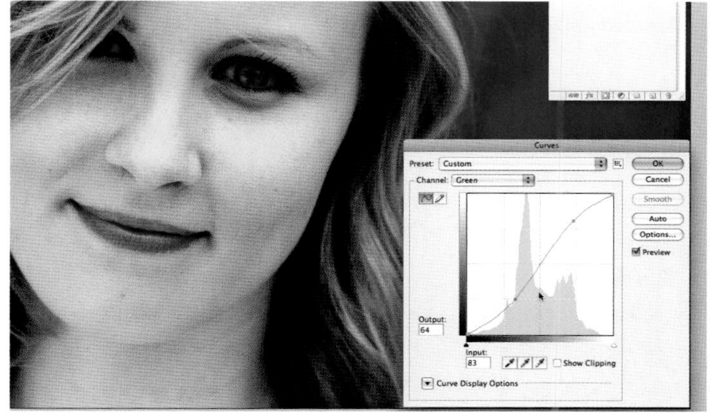

5 You can now click on the Channel tab and select Green. With the Green channel you need to select two points as you did with the Red channel, and drag them to create another gentle S curve. However, there is no need to drag the top end of the curve. You can then fine-tune the adjustments to your satisfaction. Once you are happy with the resulting image, click OK.

6 You should now have an effect that's reminiscent of a cross-processed film, with more solid, bold colours and skin tones taking on a yellow/green tinge. However, you can also create other adjustment layers to further enhance your image – in particular the Hue/Saturation and Brightness/Contrast layers, which can be selected to complete the effect to your liking.

Alternative cross-processing technique

While our main step-by-step mimics the effects of cross-processing print film in slide chemistry, many film photographers favoured experimenting with processing slide film in print (C-41) chemistry. This produced extremely high contrast images, with near-bleached white skin tones, bright red lips and very strong colours. It's a relatively easy effect to mimic by making adjustments to the Hue/Saturation and Brightness/Contrast controls in Photoshop.

1) Open the image and select *Window>Layers* to reveal the Layers palette. Select a new Adjustment Layer and choose Hue/Saturation from the drop-down menu. Boost the saturation and adjust the hue to your liking (but make sure that you don't overdo the effect!).

2) Now select a new Adjustment Layer for Brightness/Contrast and increase the contrast (and brightness if you so wish). You'll find that you start to lose detail in the highlights and shadows and the colours become far more punchy. Again, don't overdo it.

Control your contrast

MARK BAUER: One of the main technical challenges in landscape photography is controlling the contrast in a scene so that you can accurately record detail in both the land and the sky. Often the sky is a lot brighter than the land, and the contrast in the scene is beyond what the camera's sensor can record, resulting in either a well-exposed sky and underexposed foreground, or the opposite. The usual way around this is to use a Neutral Density (ND) graduated filter. These filters are brilliantly simple – they are dark at the top and clear at the bottom and all you do is position the dark half over the brighter area of the picture, reducing the contrast between the light and dark areas and therefore enabling you to capture detail in both the foreground and the sky. The only problem is that the dividing line between the dark and light areas of an ND grad is a straight line, and not all landscapes have a straight horizon – often the horizon is broken by an object such as a tree, a hill or a building, and the filter can cause an unnatural-looking darkening of the top of these objects. However, help is at hand as, most of the time, post-processing will rescue the shot. Here I explain how to use an ND Grad and remove its effect from specific areas.

1 **Arriving at Portland in Dorset just before dawn, I took a spot meter reading from the foreground rocks and the sky, which revealed a difference in brightness of around four stops. Although this falls within the dynamic range of the sensor, shadow detail has been compromised a little, and lifting this in post-processing could reveal noise in the image.**

2 **With a four-stop difference between the rocks and the sky, I chose a three-stop ND grad filter, as it would leave the sky a little bit lighter than the foreground. The next choice was to use a soft or hard grad (see panel). Soft grads aren't always the best choice for seascapes, as the brightest part of the scene is often across the horizon line, so I decided on a hard grad.**

Get ready!

TIME REQUIRED
SHOOTING: 20 MINS
PHOTOSHOP: 20 MINS

EQUIPMENT NEEDED
CANON EOS 5D MKII, 24-105MM F/4L LENS & MANFROTTO 055CLB TRIPOD

ALSO USED
REMOTE RELEASE & LEE 0.9 ND GRAD FILTER

Technique watch

HARD AND SOFT GRAD FILTERS: Neutral density graduated filters come in two varieties: hard and soft. Hard grads have a very obvious and sudden transition from the dark to clear areas, whereas soft grads have a much more gradual transition. Hard grads are more useful in situations where the horizon line is fairly straight and doesn't have any large objects breaking it. Soft grads on the other hand are a better option when you have an uneven horizon. Also, opt for a hard grad if you intend to shoot a scene with a straight horizon at sunset or sunrise, as the horizon line will be the brightest part of the scene, and soft grads won't hold back enough light.

So what do you do when you're shooting a scene at sunrise/sunset, which has a large object such as a tree or building breaking the horizon? Here's my way around this.

3 **Using the hard grad filter has resulted in a much more even exposure, but there is a problem. The top half of the lighthouse, where the filter has cut into it, is a bit too dark. The effect is fairly subtle, but it's definitely there, and doesn't look natural. Fortunately, this common problem can be easily sorted out with a spot of post-processing work.**

Final image

This is the final result, which has good detail and colour in both the sky and foreground, and a natural-looking lighthouse with no darker section at the top.

4 Using the Magnetic Lasso Tool in Photoshop, I selected the darker top half of the lighthouse, so that I could work on the problem area without affecting any other part of the image. I decided not to apply any feathering to the selection, as this could leave a 'halo' around the lighthouse once I'd finished lightening the selection.

5 There are various ways of lightening or darkening images, such as Curves and Levels, but for this selection I decided to use the Dodge Tool, as I could paint the effect on gradually and build it up in the areas that needed it more. I set the Exposure value to 10%, which enabled me to work gradually on lightening the selection.

Give your image a 1950's style appeal!

CAROLINE WILKINSON: When someone says Andy Warhol, probably one of the first images to pop into their head is a colourful montage of Marilyn Monroe or a Campbell's soup can. Warhol is one of the most recognised artists of the 1950's pop art movement and we're still replicating his style 60 years later, with a lot more ease since the introduction of Photoshop. When it comes to picking an image for a Photoshopped pop art image, it's best to pick a shot with good contrast because you'll be, in effect, using the shadows as a black outline for your colours, and without good shadow detail to define the face, your subject may look like they're without a nose or mouth. If you're unsure, check the image by turning it black & white and then clicking *Image>Adjustment>Threshold* to play with the slider to judge if enough detail is retained. You should also try to pick an image with a background that contrasts with the subject to make it easier to extract with the Magic Wand Tool. Some shots work better than others, but it's a case of trial and error. So what are you waiting for, give your shots a new lease of life with this graphic Photoshop technique.

Get ready!

TIME REQUIRED
15 MINUTES

EQUIPMENT
ADOBE PHOTOSHOP CS4

Essential tool

BE A WAND WIZARD! If you struggle selecting the whole background, increase or decrease the Tolerance level of your wand slightly and hold Shift while making multiple selections.

1 Open the image and drag the Background Layer onto the new layer icon to duplicate the layer. Now add a new coloured layer between the two layers by clicking *Layer>New Layer*, then *Edit>Fill Layer* and pick a colour. Drag this layer between the two and click the top layer.

2 Use the Magic Wand Tool to select the background and hit delete to show the coloured background behind. Go to *Select>Deselect*, then *Image>Adjustments>Desaturate* and *Image>Adjustments>Threshold*, adjusting the slider to retain facial details.

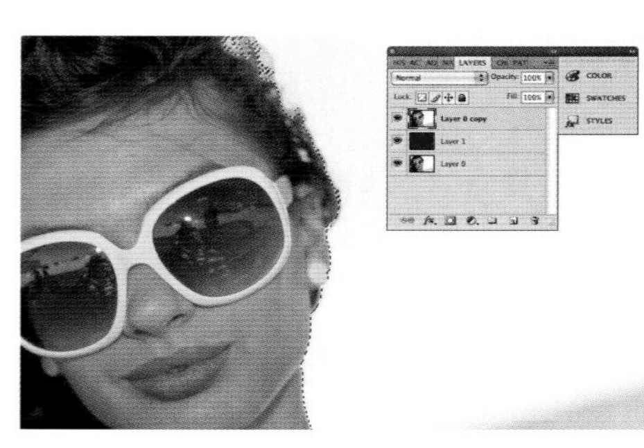

3 Add a touch of blur by going to *Filter>Blur>Gaussian Blur* and setting the slider to 1px. Drag the top layer onto the New Layer icon to duplicate. Select the Paint Bucket Tool and hit X to select a white foreground and click the face. (X changes the foreground colour from black to white).

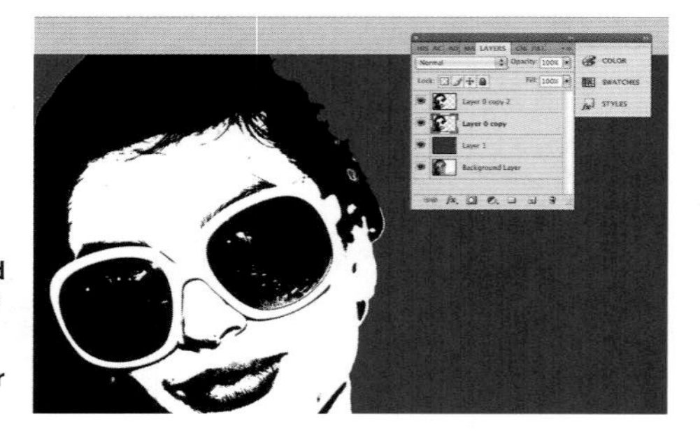

4 Select the top layer's blending mode to Multiply. Click the second layer and create a Solid adjustment layer (the split circle icon on the Layers palette). Choose a colour to use as a skin tone, then select the Paint Bucket Tool, hit X, and fill the layer with black to mask the colour.

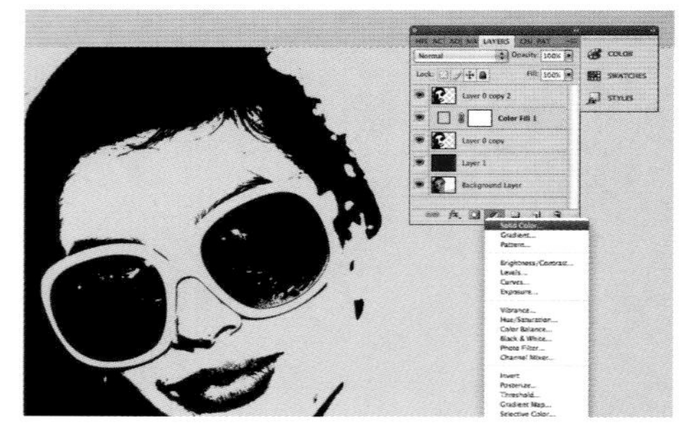

5 Hold Alt and click between the second and third layer. Now select the Brush Tool and hit X to choose a white foreground colour and paint over the skin area. Create another Solid colour adjustment layer, choose a second colour, clip the layer below and repeat for each colour.

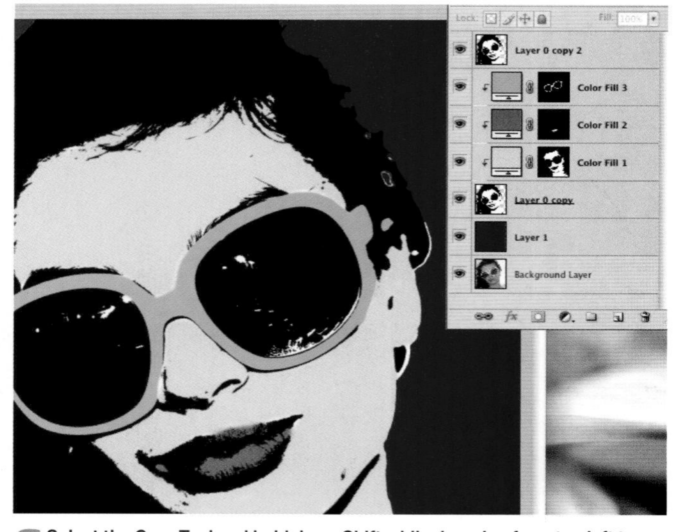

6 Select the Crop Tool and hold down Shift while dragging from top left to bottom right to create a square image. Move the square until you're happy with the crop. Double click to complete. Select all layers except the Background Layer by holding Shift and clicking on each layer.

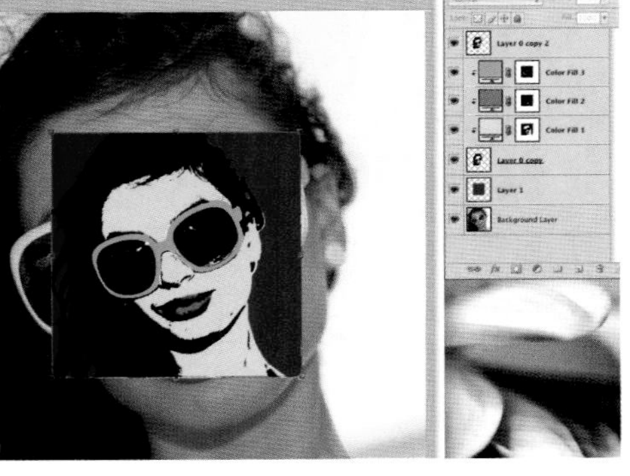

7 Hit Cmd+T to enter Free Transform. In the options at the top, change the percentages to 50% for width and height, and move the image to the top left of the picture. Select the Move Tool, hold Alt, drag the shot to the top right, making a copy of the image. Repeat three times and position the boxes on the page.

8 To change the background colours, scroll down the Layers palette to select the right layer, then choose a colour and use the Paint Bucket Tool on the square. For other features you want to change the colour of, double click on the corresponding layer's coloured box to bring up the colour picker.

Basic skills for duotones

MATT HENRY: Duotoning, otherwise known as split-toning, dates back to the days of the chemical darkroom, but with digital processing, separately toning shadows and highlights has become much quicker and easier on the wallet. The treatment suits images with good tonal range; clear distinction between the shadows and highlights, so that the colours don't overlap. There are so many colour combinations you can try: red and yellow work well, as do green and blue, but the effect can also be changed depending on which colour you use for highlights and which you use for shadows. For instance, red highlights and blue shadows give a contemporary, energising look, while red shadows and blue highlights can be more unsettling. There are no hard and fast rules though – keep mixing it up until you hit on something you like.

Get ready!

TIME REQUIRED
15 MINUTES

EQUIPMENT
ADOBE PHOTOSHOP CS4

Technique watch

TO BLEND OR NOT TO BLEND?
Although there are different ways to achieve the duotone effect in Photoshop, Blending Options offer by far the most control over results. You can be selective, using the sliders to specify which tones receive the colour wash and those that don't: making it easier to keep colours separate as is often the danger with other techniques. Blending Options aren't accessible for Elements users but excellent results can still be achieved using Color Variations and selecting shadows and highlights separately.

1 The first thing to do is convert our image to mono. Elements users should duplicate the Background Layer with Ctrl/Cmd+J and run *Enhance>Convert to Black & White*. Photoshop users should add a Black & White adjustment layer using the button at the layer palette base (or Layer>New Adjustment Layer).

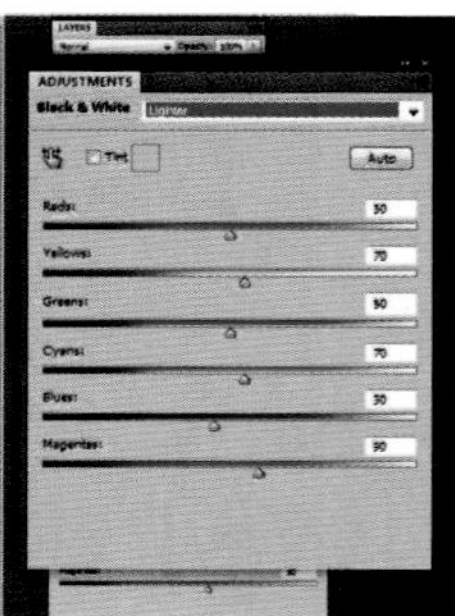

2 In both Adobe Elements and Photoshop, you have the option to choose one of the presets (use the drop-down menu in Photoshop) or work with the colour sliders to produce the desired effect. Experiment freely with each method until you reach a look that suits the particular image in hand.

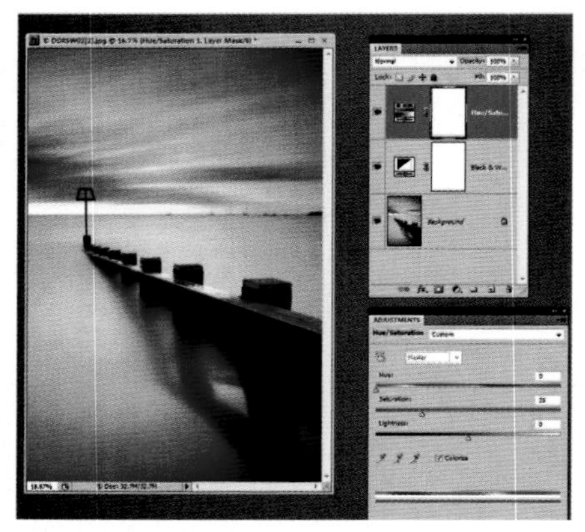

3 Once the image is converted to black & white, in Photoshop, add a Hue/Saturation adjustment layer and check the box that says Colorize. Before we go any further, change the layer's blending mode from Normal to Color using the drop-down menu to prevent the image being lightened or darkened.

4 Drag the Hue slider to establish the colour wash you'd like for the shadows. Ignore the fact that the colour is applied to the whole tonal range for now. Select the Hue/Saturation layer and select *Layer>Layer Style>Blending Options*. Hold Alt and click the white triangle on the This Layer slider to split it into two parts.

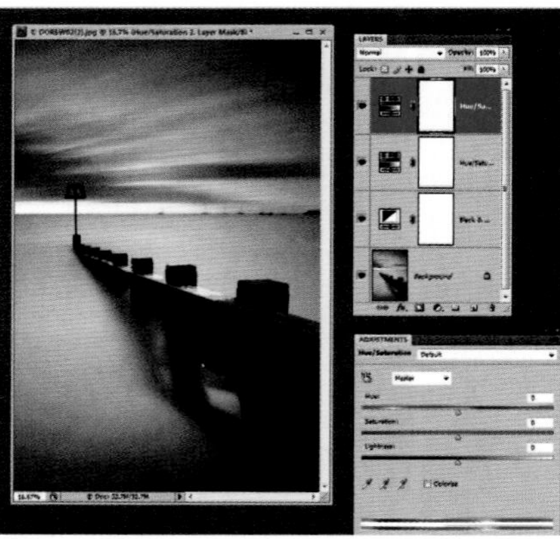

5 Now, drag the left-hand part of the triangle along to the 100 setting and the right-hand part to 175. If you now click the Preview box on and off you can see how the highlight tones have been excluded from the toning. Click *OK* then add another Hue/Saturation adjustment layer, checking the Colorize box again.

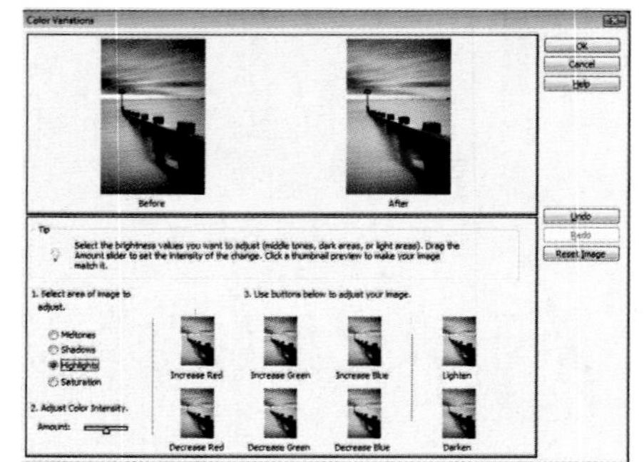

6 Change the layer blending mode from Normal to Color and move the Hue slider to choose your highlight colour. Click *Layer>Layer Style>Blending Options* and split the black triangle. Set the right side to 155 and the left to 80. Click *OK* to finish the Photoshop work.

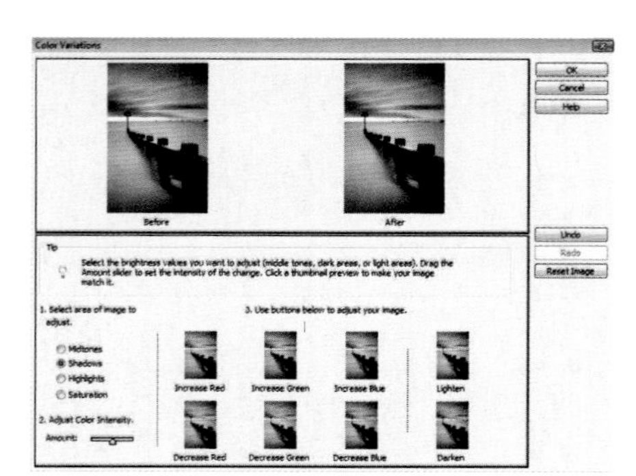

7 Elements users don't have the luxury of blending options so we need to use Variations. Go to *Enhance>Adjust Color>Color Variations*. Now select Shadows on the left to start and click the relevant picture button to add the colour of your choice to the shadows.

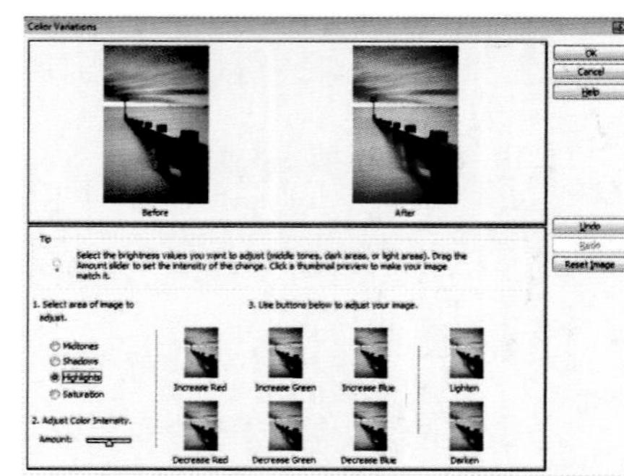

8 Click as many times as you need to get the desired strength, and don't be afraid to mix colour tones to get the right effect. Use the subtract picture button if you go too far. Check the Highlight button when you're done and repeat for the highlight tones. Click *OK* to finish.

Final image
As you can see, the Photoshop treatment has given the former black & white image a new and appealing atmosphere.

Outdoor
Indoor
Lighting
Creative
Photoshop

Add an artistic edge

CAROLINE WILKINSON: When shooting a portrait there is a lot we can do to control key elements such as poses, lighting and composition. But there are also many instances when you can't control it all. For example, this bridal portrait had great lighting coming from the window but the backdrop was cluttered and distracting – ruining the photograph. Often, you can add blur in Photoshop to recreate a shallow depth-of-field, softening the imposing background. But in this case, it's not enough and for this picture to be a success the backdrop needs to be simplified. Using a coloured layer to mask the background is an effective way of transforming most images that have great light but a messy backdrop. If you have images with a similar problem, then give this technique a try!

Get ready!

TIME REQUIRED 30 MINUTES

EQUIPMENT NEEDED PHOTOSHOP CS3

Brushes & layers!

This technique requires you to create a new 'black' layer and use the Paint Brush Tool to remove the colour and reveal the image underneath. A fair amount of trial and error is needed to get an even result, but one way is to keep a soft medium-sized, very low-opacity brush moving and gradually strip away the colour. If you do make a mistake, change the brush Mode to Darken and go over the areas where the opacity is too thin.

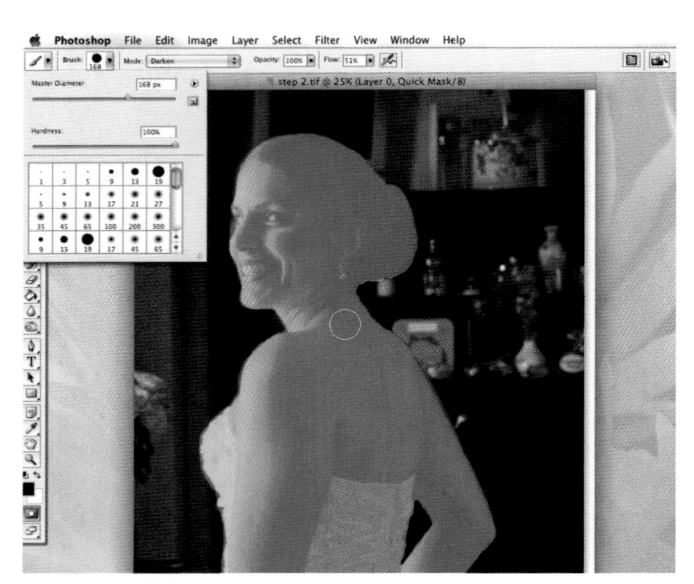

1 I tried to blur the background by masking off the bride and applying the maximum lens blur to the background by using *Filter>Blur>Lens Blur* and setting the Radius to 100%. I wanted a simple image that focused on the bride and lighting; this technique didn't do that.

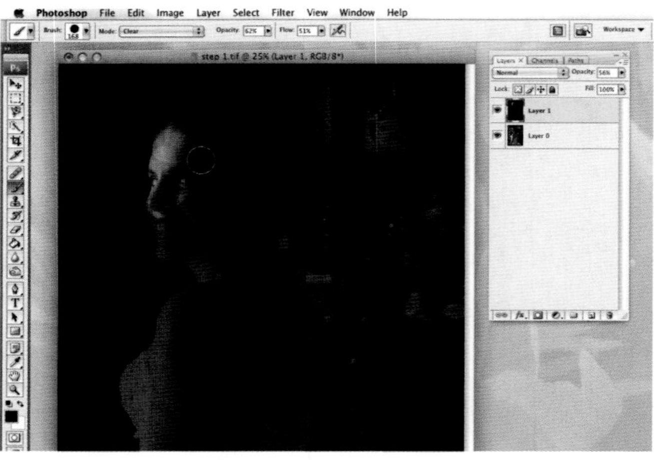

2 I made a second layer (*Layer>New>Layer*) and, with the Paint Bucket Tool, coloured it black. I brought the opacity of the layer down to 56% so as to see the image underneath and, using the Clear brush mode and opacity of 62%, started to erase areas I wanted to reveal.

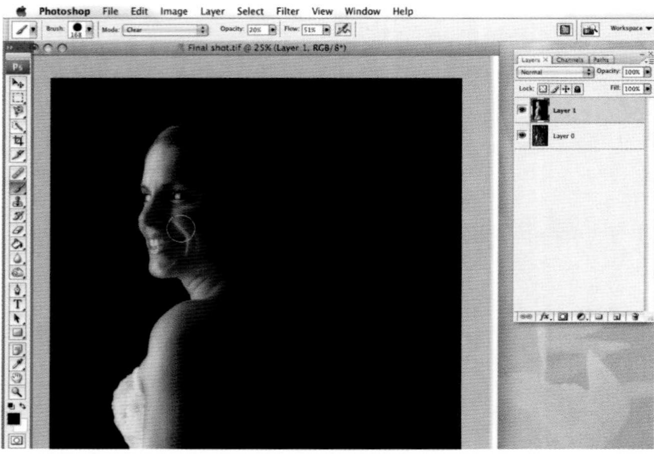

3 It's worth playing around with the different brush modes, sizes and opacities to get the desired effect. I found that 62% was too harsh to get a smooth finish and I got a better result with the layer's opacity at 100% and by varying the brush opacity between 9 and 17%.

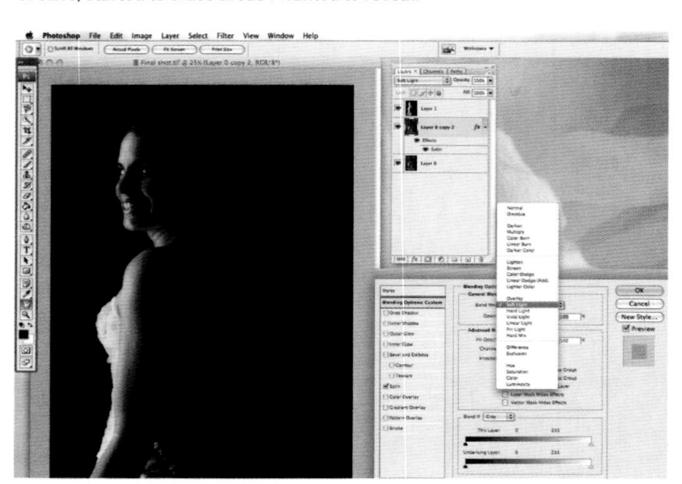

4 Once I was happy with the detail I'd brought forward, I felt that the graduation between the bride's profile and the black fill layer needed to be smoother, so I played with the different blending options (*Layer>Layer Style*). The Satin blend gave me the smoothest finish.

5 Each Blend Option has a range of Blend Modes to experiment with. I was tempted to use Soft Light as it boosted the bride's glow and contrast, but in the end I opted for the Normal setting as it offered a less stark result with more natural skin tones, which suited my image better.

Keep it simple
Pick a subject that has a good tonal range and concentrate on bringing the opacity of the highlights back to 100%, especially the whites of eyes, so you create an image high in contrast

Final image

You may find that adding a blending option boosts the shadows, so it's worth going back over areas of the subject with a low opacity brush to recover the details. To make this image even simpler, I added a black & white adjustment layer (*Adjustments>Black & White*) and using the Darken brush mode, I went over areas of the black layer where the opacity had been reduced.

Boost contrast with blending modes

CAROLINE WILKINSON: Manipulating contrast and colour saturation is what Adobe Photoshop excels at, but these two properties are often interlinked. Boost an image's contrast and you'll notice the colours may look oversaturated too. While adjusting the Levels or Curves is the most common way to change contrast and the Hue/Saturation tool for adjusting colour, using blending modes in a multi-layered image can be quicker and give you more creative flexibility.

Put simply, blending modes determine how a top layer interacts, or 'blends' with the layer underneath. There are 25 blending modes to pick from, each having a different effect, but there is also a group dedicated to changing contrast, including Soft Light, Hard Light, Linear Light, Hard Mix and, one of the most used, Overlay. Each one handles light and dark differently – so it's worth experimenting – and it's worth noting that you can add them to any layer: a duplicate layer, an adjustment layer, a fill layer or a different image layer.

If you are new to working with multiple layers and blending modes, don't be daunted, this may sound advanced but it's not. In fact, this tutorial could be the encouragement you need to start using layers in all of your Photoshop and Elements editing. Let's see how it's done.

Get ready!

TIME REQUIRED
TEN MINUTES

EQUIPMENT NEEDED
ADOBE PHOTOSHOP OR ELEMENTS

Finding Layer Blend Modes

While you can go to ***Layer>Layer Style>Blending Options*** and find the Blend Mode drop-down menu under General Blending, along with many other advanced options that will look very confusing to you at this stage, there's a much quicker way. All the blend modes can be found on a drop-down list in the top-left corner of the Layers palette, which by default will have Normal blend mode selected.

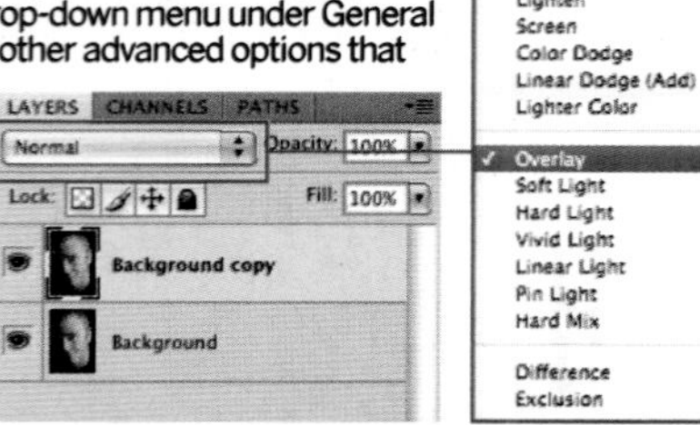

1 You need at least two layers for this technique to work, as a blend mode determines how a top layer interacts with the layer underneath it. So, to begin with, I duplicate the Background Layer, by clicking the layer and choosing *Layer>Duplicate Layer* or *Ctrl+J*.

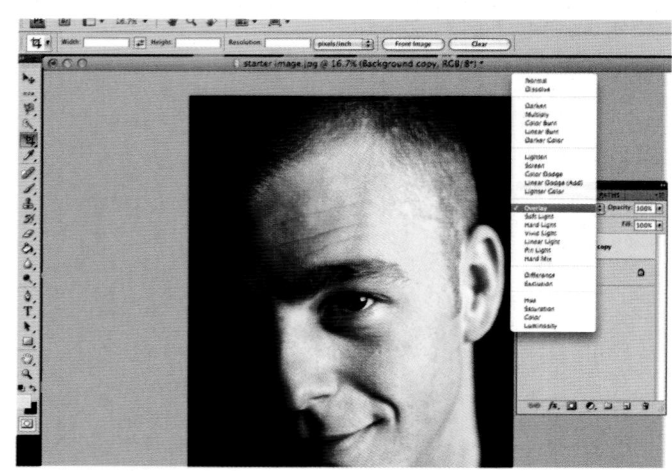

2 I want to boost the contrast, so I run through the list of blend modes and finally opt for Overlay, as it darkens the blacks and lightens the highlights. If the effect is too strong, try reducing the top layer's opacity. By boosting the contrast, however, I've oversaturated the face, making it red.

3 I need to separate the contrast and saturation, so sticking with Overlay and at opacity 100%, I take the colour out of the top layer using the command *Image>Adjustments>Desaturate*. It's given me the boost in contrast I want and muted the colours. I like it!

4 By desaturing the shot, I've lost the colour in the eye. To give it back its impact, I have used a Quick Mask and small brush to select the eye on the Background Layer. Click the Quick Mask icon again to reveal marching ants. I then boost the colour (*Image>Adjustments>Hue/Saturation*).

Quick fix
Overlay is a combination of Multiply and Screen blend modes. Use them separately to darken or lighten images, respectively. Great if you're dealing with over or underexposed photos

Final image
Overall, I'm happy with the final image, but thought it was a bit soft, so I added a High Pass filter to boost the detail. I did this by duplicating the Background Layer again, and making it the top layer, then adding a High Pass filter *(Filter>Other>High Pass)* set to 5 pixels and selecting the blending mode to Overlay. Experiment with different filters and blending modes for various creative effects.

Create a fun 'face-flip'

MAT GALLAGHER: It is often thought that the more symmetrical your face is, the more pleasing or beautiful you appear. This is why you'll find that most models and film stars have very symmetrical features. Most of us however, aren't blessed with mirror perfect symmetry but with the help of a little Photoshop work, we can see what we'd look like if we were. This technique is in essence, the digital equivalent to standing at right angles to mirrored glass in a hall of mirrors, as it duplicates one side of your face onto the other and can have some very bizarre effects. The first stage is to take a photo of your subject, or of yourself if you want to flip a self-portrait. For best results, ensure that the lighting is even across the face, and not just coming in from one side. Make sure that you shoot the face straight on and from a level height, as any kind of angle will distort the effect. If however, you want to create some more whacky effects, ignore these guidelines and have some fun!

For my image, I used a studio shot that I'd taken earlier in the week. It was taken against a white background and straight on to the camera, thus making the process easy. It's best to do any alterations and cloning work to the face before you do the mirror flip, as any imperfections will appear twice once you've flipped it. The Healing Brush tool makes this quick and easy, while the Paintbrush tool on a low opacity and flow, with a sampled colour, can be used over larger areas.

One of the great things about this technique is that, even on a seemingly even face, you can end up with two very different-looking images from the left and right sides. You can then pick the version you prefer or place them next to each other to show the difference. After a quick trial run, I choose to use the left-hand-side of my model's face as it gave a nicer result. If the image is pretty straight to start with and sliced in carefully, the joining process should be hassle-free with little adjustment needed. The main areas to watch though are the hairline and the neck – you may get a light or dark line along the 'seam' too but this can be easily removed with some careful cloning or healing brush work.

Original

Get ready!

TIME REQUIRED
1 HOUR 15 MINUTES

EQUIPMENT USED
ADOBE ELEMENTS

ALSO USED
SYMMETRICAL PORTRAIT

Essential kit

PHOTO EDITING SOFTWARE: Though you may aspire to have the very latest version of Adobe Photoshop CS for your image editing, you can still achieve some impressive results with more modest software packages. The basic adjustment tools that you need to tweak your images haven't changed that much over the years, and this tutorial along with many others we will cover in the mag can be followed with just about any photo editing software. We have used Adobe Elements 4.0 to create the images and screen grabs here, to show just how simple it is. If you don't currently have any photo editing software, or are looking to upgrade your current software, we recommend you look at Adobe Elements 10, which offers plenty of features at an affordable price.

1 To check the model's head is straight, select the Crop tool from the tools palette, click and drag to create a box, then line up the edge of the box with the line of the nose and the centre of the lips. If this line isn't straight, click and drag outside of the box to rotate until it is. Now expand the edges of the Crop to fit the rest of the image in and double click inside the box to accept.

2 Now your image is straight, select the Rectangular Marquee tool from the tools palette and (depending on which side of the face you want to use) click and drag from the top left or top right corner, down to the bottom centre, so the edge of the selection goes through the centre of the nose and lips. Now press Ctrl+J to paste the selection into a duplicate layer.

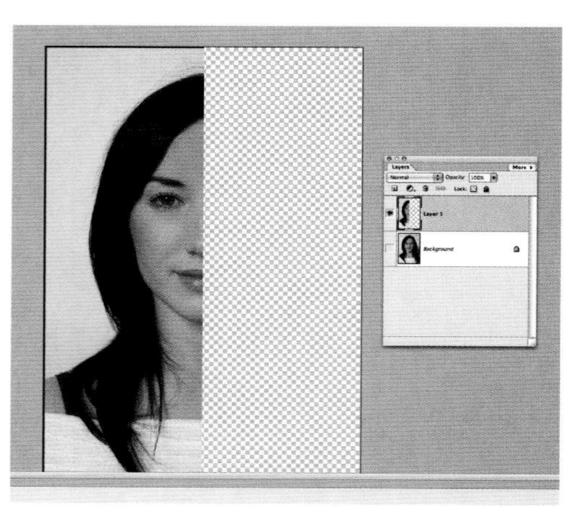

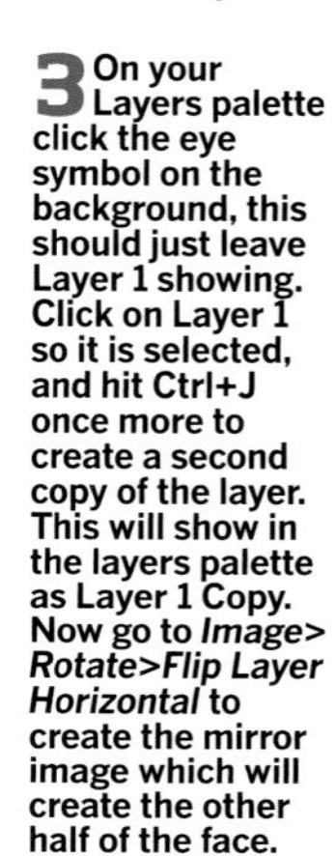

3 On your Layers palette click the eye symbol on the background, this should just leave Layer 1 showing. Click on Layer 1 so it is selected, and hit Ctrl+J once more to create a second copy of the layer. This will show in the layers palette as Layer 1 Copy. Now go to *Image>Rotate>Flip Layer Horizontal* to create the mirror image which will create the other half of the face.

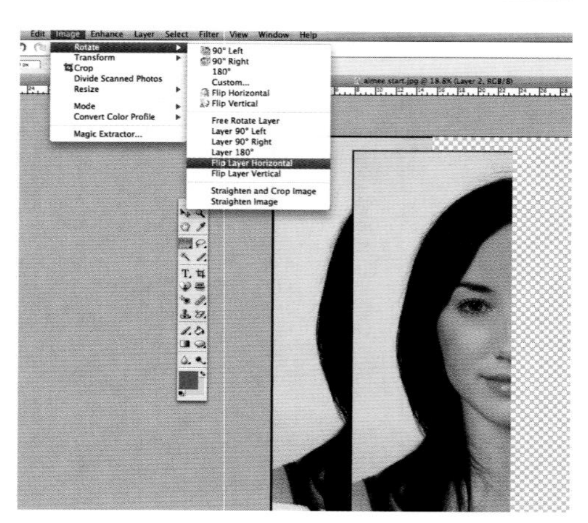

4 Make sure you have your new top layer selected in the layers palette. Now select the Move tool from the tools palette, then click and drag the layer to align it with the other half of the face. Check that it lines up correctly by zooming in on details around the lips or nose and fine-tuning them. Once you're happy, hit Ctrl+E to 'Merge down', combining it with the layer below.

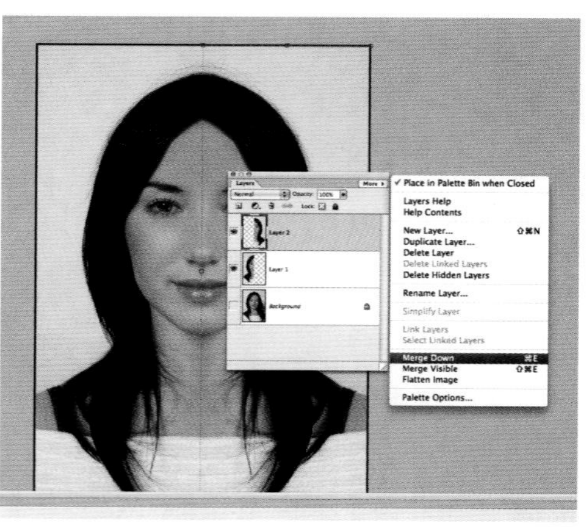

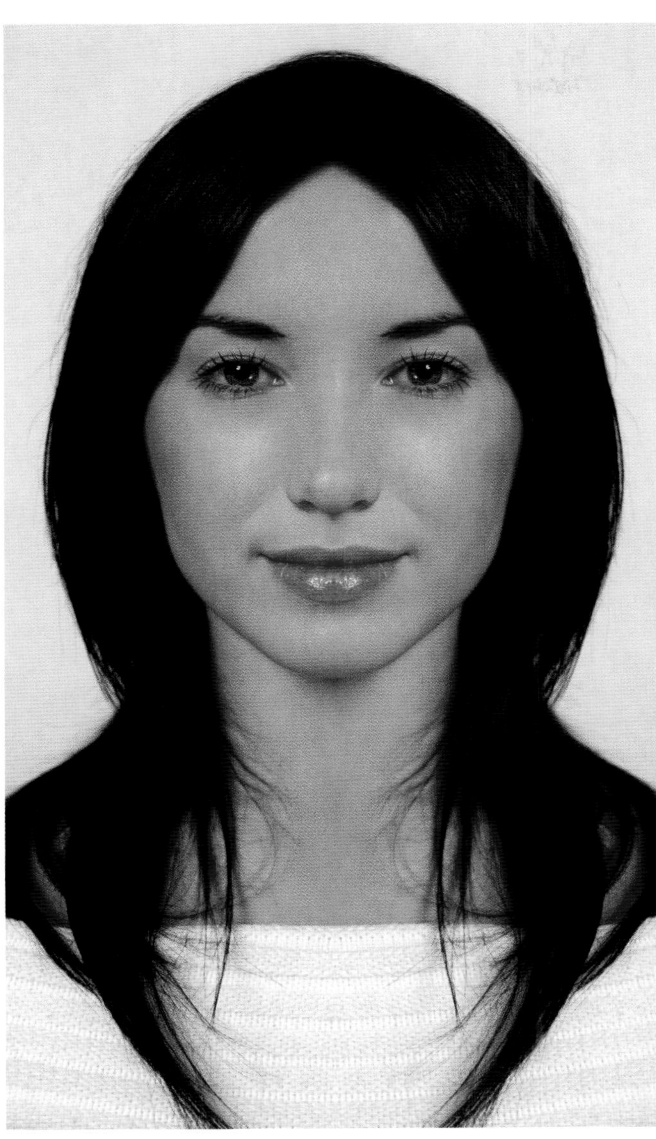

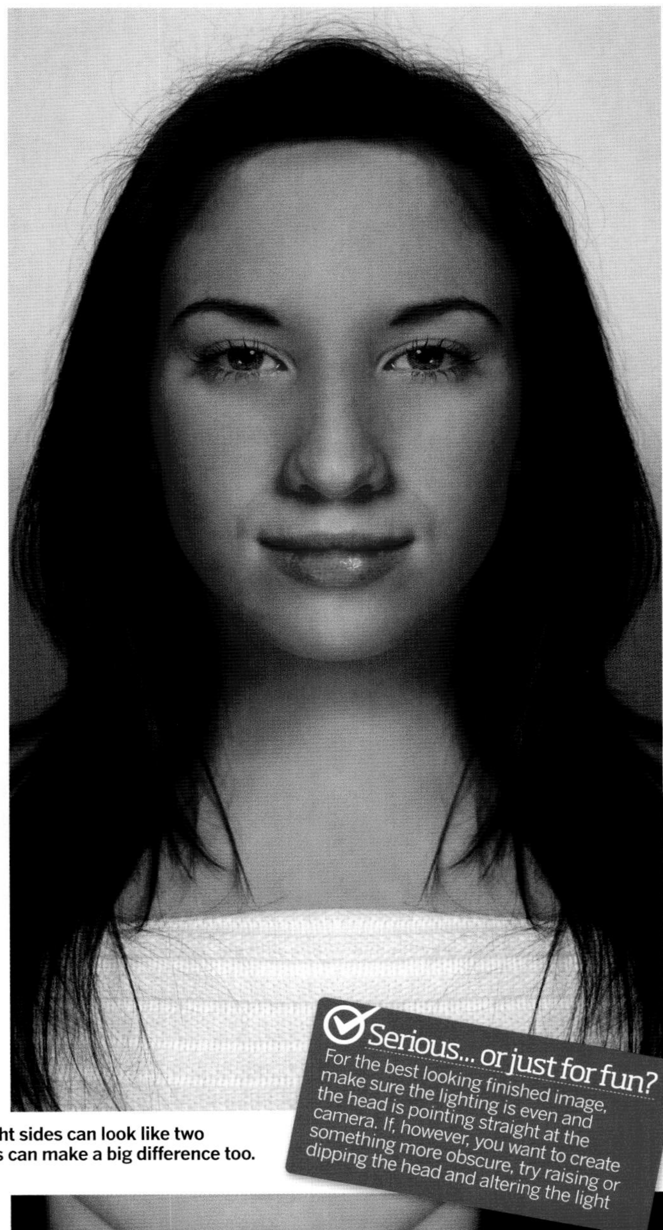

Serious... or just for fun?
For the best looking finished image, make sure the lighting is even and the head is pointing straight at the camera. If, however, you want to create something more obscure, try raising or dipping the head and altering the light

FINAL IMAGE: Even with quite a symmetrical face, the results from the left and right sides can look like two different people. As you can see, unless the model has a symmetrical hair line, this can make a big difference too.

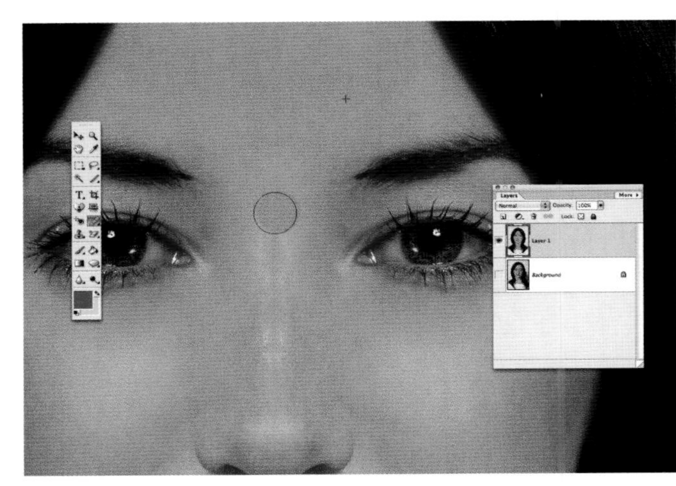

5 If your starting image was well-lit, you shouldn't have too much work to do here, though hair and neck-lines may need some extra attention. Select the Healing Brush from the tools palette, then hold Alt and Click to select a sample point from a smooth area of skin, then paint over problem areas with small strokes, using a small to medium-sized, soft edged brush.

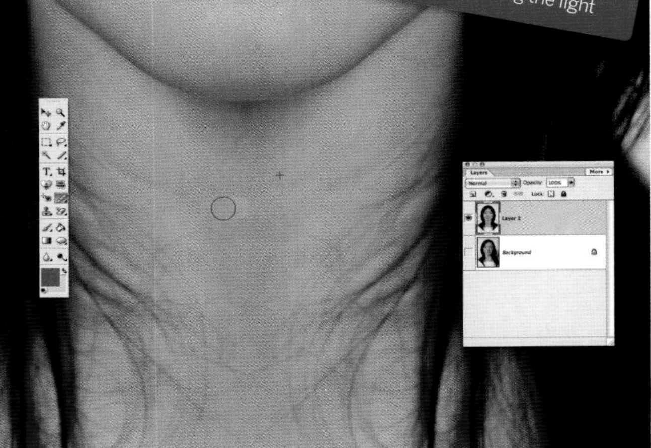

6 Work your way down the seam to remove the light or dark strip that often occurs along the joint. Be patient with the neckline, as shadows cast by the chin and longer hair can prove problematic. Once you are happy, save your image under a new name, then try using the same technique for the other side of the face to make a set, or create a flip-face of each family member.

It's toy town time!

MATTY GRAHAM: How do you turn a city scene into a toy town? This increasingly fashionable style of photography, using shallow depth-of-field, selective focusing and saturated colours, is known as 'tilt shift' and is normally achieved through the use of dedicated lenses, but we're going to show you how to create the effect for yourself in Photoshop. Miniature scenes are usually viewed from above, which means that miniature photography works best on images shot from a high vantage point, like a bridge or building. Thanks to a combination of selective blur and saturation, you can bring a standard shot to life, and make it appear more like a child's playset. If you're new to Photoshop, it may take some trial and error to get the effect right, but once you do, you'll be addicted!

Get ready!

TIME REQUIRED
20 MINUTES

EQUIPMENT NEEDED
PHOTOSHOP (CS3+)

Technique watch

PHOTOSHOP'S BLUR FILTERS:
You can find several different filters in the Blur section, but the most popular are Lens, Motion and Gaussian blur. These tools can be used to smooth skin in a portrait, add motion to a static subject, eliminate dust or fluff, soften print texture or give a shallow depth-of-field effect.

1 Open your image in Photoshop and select the Quick Mask Mode, which is a circle icon on your Tools palette. If you can't find it, just press Q on your keyboard instead.

2 Select the Brush Tool from your Tools palette. Draw a horizontal line across the screen, covering the area you want to remain sharp in the image. Use a soft brush at 85% opacity.

3 If you don't have Quick Mask Mode, choose the Gradient tool option by either pressing G on your keyboard, or selecting it from your Tools palette. As before, draw your line across the screen where you want the image to remain sharp.

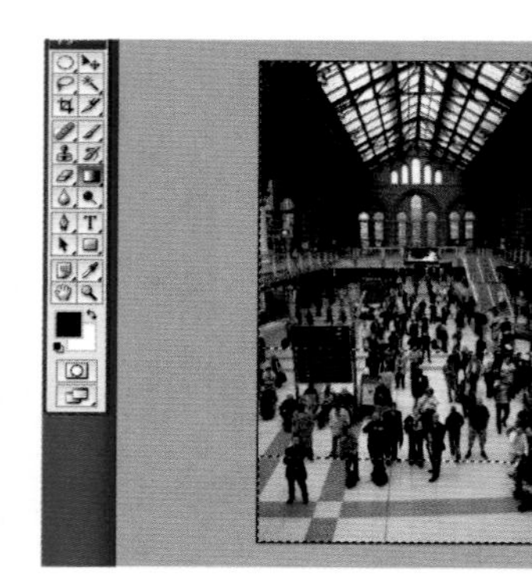

4 You should now see where you've applied your mask area. If it isn't right, just go back and repeat the last step. If you're happy with you mask area, press Q. The mask area will now be surrounded by 'marching ants'.

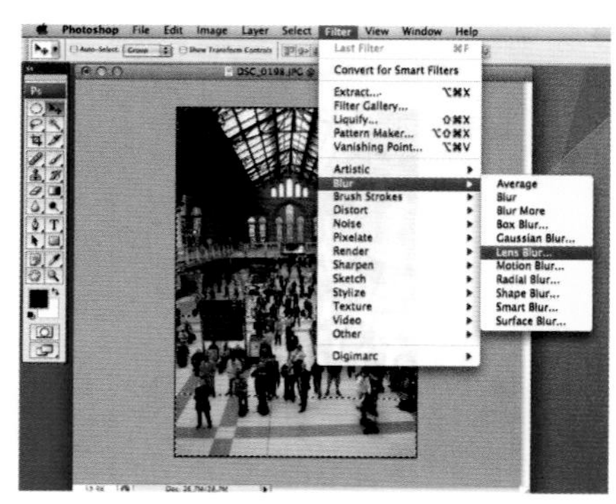

5 It's time to apply the all-important blur to the image now. Click on *Filter>Blur>Lens Blur* and you will now see the effect applied to your image in a preview panel. Tweak the blur options until you're happy and then click *OK*!

6 Click Ctrl+D to remove the 'marching ants' and you're ready to adjust the saturation. Go to *Image>Adjustments>Hue/Saturation*, or click (Ctrl+U) to bring up the Saturation option.

7 You need to boost the Saturation by dragging the middle slider to the right. This step is down to personal taste, but we'd recommend changing the amount to around +40.

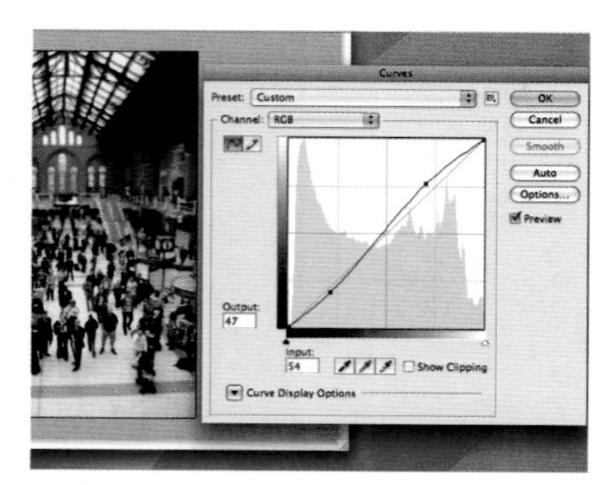

8 Select curves (Ctrl+M) and move the curve line into a small S-shape. Be careful not to overdo this function as it may spoil your image. Save your image (*File>Save*).

First Class lounge
Left luggage
Accessible toilets
Taxis

Pick a colour, create a poster!

Get ready!

TIME REQUIRED
TWO HOURS

EQUIPMENT NEEDED
CANON EOS-1Ds MkIII, 24-70MM ZOOM

ALSO USED
PHOTOSHOP CS3

LEE FROST: While leading a photo workshop on the Northumberland coast recently, my group and I had to face the inevitable dull day that's par for the course when shooting landscapes in the UK. Luckily, we were on the Holy Island of Lindisfarne, which is packed with details that suit the soft light created by overcast weather, so I set everyone the task of seeking out and shooting details in the fishermen's huts, old boats, lobster pots and piles of fish crates. No individual shot would be a masterpiece, but as a set of images they would gain collective visual strength. To prove this, I started shooting details in the steel hull of a yacht that had been painted bright blue. I then started looking for other blue subjects scattered around the harbour and before I knew it, I'd created an eye-catching set of themed images. Back home, Raw files processed, all I had to do was decide what to do with them and the idea of a colourful poster came to mind. Here's a step-by-step to how I created it.

GETTING THE SHOTS: To photograph images for this poster project, I used one camera and one lens – my trusty 24-70mm standard zoom, which has a decent close-focusing capability. Although I normally use a tripod for just about every shot, on this occasion I wanted to be able to move around quickly and freely, so I decided to shoot handheld. As the weather was dull and light levels relatively low compared to a sunny day, I increased the ISO to 400 in order to maintain a reasonably fast shutter speed and prevent camera shake.

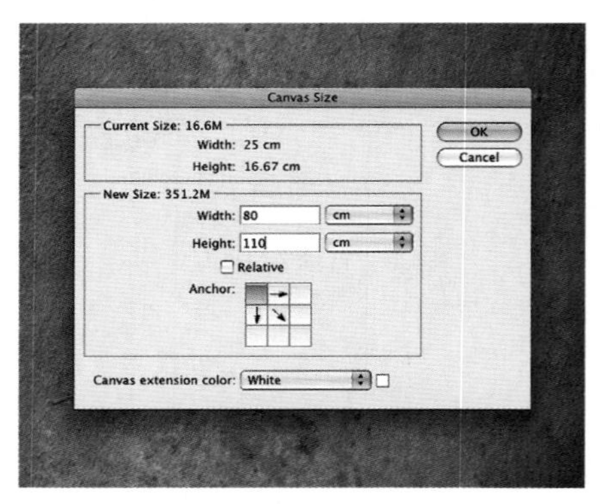

1 Process the Raw files then make JPEG copies of your selected images. Using the JPEG format reduces the size of each image so that when you combine a dozen or more of them the resulting file size doesn't make your computer blow a gasket! I also reduced the image size so each image was 25cm wide at 300dpi.

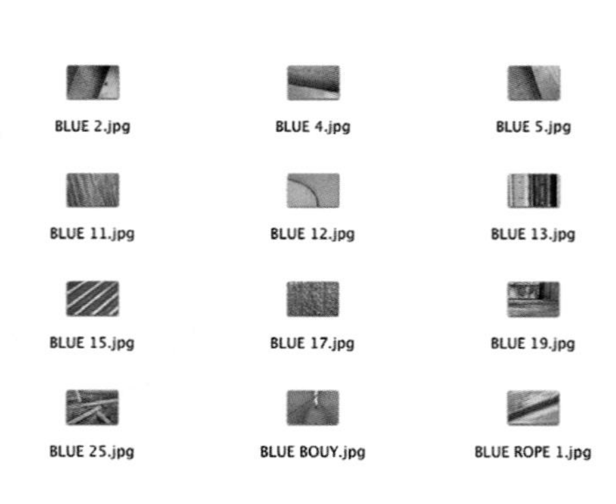

2 Open the first image in the montage and increase the size of the canvas so it's big enough to add all other images in the set. My montage will be three images wide by six deep, so 80x110cm should be OK. You can always make the canvas bigger at a later stage, or crop any excess canvas. I placed my first image in the top left corner.

3 Double click your second image, then using the Move Tool in Photoshop, drag and drop the image onto the enlarged canvas. You can use the Move Tool to position the image next to the first one and the Arrow Keys to then fine-tune the position of the image. I chose to leave a gap between each image.

4 Repeat step three, dragging, dropping and positioning each image on the canvas. If you need to make changes to any of the images, open the Layers (*Windows>Layers*), click on the appropriate layer and do what needs to be done. Remember to save the montage as you go.

5 With all images in place, crop any excess canvas then go to *Layer>Flatten Image* to merge the layers. Add a border by extending the canvas using *Image>Canvas Size* and increasing it evenly on all four sides. Select *Image>Canvas* again but only extend the bottom edge so that you can add text.

6 Click on the Type Tool icon in Photoshop then drag the cursor across the bottom border of the poster to create a text box. Next, add a title and your name, then experiment with different type sizes and typefaces until you're happy. Finally, choose the colour of the text if you don't want plain black.

MOODY BLUES

Lee Frost